64

ASPECTS OF THE NOVEL

November 1998

Happy Birthday Ray

Love,

Bonnie & Dad

LETS HOPE APRIL 15TH IS THE FIRST OF MANY!!

E. M. Forster, one of England's most distinguished writers, was born in 1879 and attended King's College, Cambridge, of which he was an honorary Fellow. He was named to membership in the Order of Companions of Honor by the Queen in 1953. He wrote his first novel, *Where Angels Fear to Tread,* at twenty-six, followed by *A Room with a View* in 1908, *Howards End* in 1910, and other novels and critical essays. These include *A Passage to India* (1924), *Aspects of the Novel* (1927), *Abinger Harvest* (1936), *Two Cheers for Democracy* (1951), *The Hill of Devi* (1953), and *Marianne Thornton,* the biography of his great-aunt (1956). Two books have been published since his death in 1970: *Maurice* (1972) and *The Life to Come and Other Stories* (1973).

E. M. FORSTER

Aspects of the Novel

A HARVEST BOOK
HARCOURT BRACE & COMPANY
SAN DIEGO NEW YORK LONDON

Library of Congress Cataloging-in-Publication Data
Forster, E. M. (Edward Morgan), 1879–1970.
Aspects of the novel.
"A Harvest book."
1. Fiction. 2. English fiction—History and criticism. I. Title.
PN3353.F6 1985 808.3 84-22498
ISBN 0-15-609180-1 (pbk.)

Printed in the United States of America
NN PP OO MM

To
CHARLES MAURON

Note

THESE are some lectures (the Clark lectures) which were delivered under the auspices of Trinity College, Cambridge, in the spring of 1927. They were informal, indeed talkative, in their tone, and it seemed safer when presenting them in book form not to mitigate the talk, in case nothing should be left at all. Words such as "I," "you," "one," "we," "curiously enough," "so to speak," "only imagine," and "of course" will consequently occur on every page and will rightly distress the sensitive reader; but he is asked to remember that if these words were removed others, perhaps more distinguished, might escape through the orifices they left, and that since the novel is itself often colloquial it may possibly withhold some of its secrets from the graver and grander streams of criticism, and may reveal them to backwaters and shallows.

The text of this reissue of Mr. Forster's brilliant discussion is unchanged from the original edition of 1927. No attempt has been made to bring up to date the few topical references, mainly in footnotes, affected by the passage of time.

Contents

ASPECTS OF THE NOVEL

One

INTRODUCTORY

THIS lectureship is connected with the name of William George Clark, a fellow of Trinity. It is through him we meet today, and through him we shall approach our subject.

Clark was, I believe, a Yorkshireman. He was born in 1821, was at school at Sedbergh and Shrewsbury, entered Trinity as an undergraduate in 1840, became fellow four years later, and made the college his home for nearly thirty years, only leaving it when his health broke, shortly before his death. He is best known as a Shakespearian scholar, but he published two books on other subjects to which we must here refer. He went as a young man to Spain and wrote a pleasant lively account of his holiday called *Gazpacho:* Gazpacho being the name of a certain cold soup which he ate and appears to have enjoyed among the peasants of Andalusia: indeed he appears to have enjoyed everything. Eight years later, as a result of a holiday in Greece, he published a second book, *Peloponnesus. Peloponnesus* is a graver work and a duller. Greece was a serious place in those days, more serious than Spain, besides, Clark had by now not only taken Orders but become Public Orator, and he was, above all, travelling with Dr. Thompson, the then Master of the college, who was not at all the sort of person to be involved in a cold soup. The jests about mules and fleas are consequently few, and we are increasingly confronted with the remains of Classical Antiquity and the sites of battles. What survives in the book—apart from its learning—is its feeling for Greek countryside. Clark also travelled in Italy and Poland.

To turn to his academic career. He planned the great *Cambridge Shakespeare,* first with Glover, then with Aldis Wright (both librarians of Trinity), and, helped by Aldis Wright, he issued the *Globe Shakespeare,* a popular text. He collected much material for an edition of Aristophanes. He also published some sermons, but in 1869 he gave up Holy Orders—which, by the way, will exempt us from excessive orthodoxy. Like his friend and biographer Leslie Stephen, like Henry Sidgwick and others of that generation, he did not find it possible to remain in the Church, and he has explained his reasons in a pamphlet entitled *The Present Dangers of the Church of England.* He resigned his post of Public Orator in consequence, while retaining his college tutorship. He died at the age of fifty-seven, esteemed by all who knew him as a lovable, scholarly and honest man. You will have realized that he is a Cambridge figure. Not a figure in the great world or even at Oxford, but a spirit peculiar to these courts, which perhaps only you who tread them after him can justly appreciate: the spirit of integrity. Out of a bequest in his will, his old college has provided for a series of lectures, to be delivered annually "on some period or periods of English Literature not earlier than Chaucer," and that is why we meet here now.

Invocations are out of fashion, yet I wanted to make this small one, for two reasons. Firstly, may a little of Clark's integrity be with us through this course; and secondly, may he accord us a little inattention! For I am not keeping quite strictly to the terms laid down—"Period or periods of English Literature." This condition, though it sounds liberal and is liberal enough in spirit, happens verbally not quite to suit our subject, and I shall occupy the introductory lecture in explaining why this is. The points raised may seem trivial. But they will lead us to a convenient vantage post from which we can begin our main attack next week.

We need a vantage post, for the novel is a formidable mass, and it is so amorphous—no mountain in it to climb, no Parnassus or Helicon, not even a Pisgah. It is most distinctly one of the moister areas of literature—irrigated by a hundred rills and occasionally degenerating into a swamp. I do not wonder that the poets despise it, though they sometimes find themselves in it by accident. And I am not surprised at the annoyance of the historians when by accident it finds itself among them. Perhaps we ought to define what a novel is before starting. This will not take a second. M. Abel Chevalley has, in his brilliant little manual,[1] provided a definition, and if a French critic cannot define the English novel, who can? It is, he says, "a fiction in prose of a certain extent" (*une fiction en prose d'une certaine étendue*). That is quite good enough for us, and we may perhaps go so far as to add that the extent should not be less than 50,000 words. Any fictitious prose work over 50,000 words will be a novel for the purposes of these lectures, and if this seems to you unphilosophic will you think of an alternative definition, which will include *The Pilgrim's Progress, Marius the Epicurean, The Adventures of a Younger Son, The Magic Flute, The Journal of the Plague, Zuleika Dobson, Rasselas, Ulysses,* and *Green Mansions,* or else will give reasons for their exclusion? Parts of our spongy tract seem more fictitious than other parts, it is true: near the middle, on a tump of grass, stand Miss Austen with the figure of Emma by her side, and Thackeray holding up Esmond. But no intelligent remark known to me will define the tract as a whole. All we can say of it is that it is bounded by two chains of mountains neither of which rises very abruptly—the opposing ranges of Poetry and of History—and bounded on the third side by a sea—a sea that we shall encounter when we come to *Moby Dick*.

Let us begin by considering the proviso "English Literature." "English" we shall of course interpret as written in English, not as published south of the

[1] Abel Chevalley, *Le Roman Anglais de Notre Temps,* Oxford University Press, New York.

Tweed or east of the Atlantic, or north of the Equator: we need not attend to geographical accidents, they can be left to the politicians. Yet, even with this interpretation, are we as free as we wish? Can we, while discussing English fiction, quite ignore fiction written in other languages, particularly French and Russian? As far as influence goes, we could ignore it, for our writers have never been much influenced by the continentals. But—for reasons soon to be explained—I want to talk as little as possible about influence during these lectures. My subject is a particular kind of book and the aspects that book has assumed in English. Can we ignore its collateral aspects on the continent? Not entirely. An unpleasant and unpatriotic truth has here to be faced. No English novelist is as great as Tolstoy—that is to say has given so complete a picture of man's life, both on its domestic and heroic side. No English novelist has explored man's soul as deeply as Dostoevsky. And no novelist anywhere has analysed the modern consciousness as successfully as Marcel Proust. Before these triumphs we must pause. English poetry fears no one—excels in quality as well as quantity. But English fiction is less triumphant: it does not contain the best stuff yet written, and if we deny this we become guilty of provincialism.

Now, provincialism does not signify in a writer, and may indeed be the chief source of his strength: only a prig or a fool would complain that Defoe is cockneyfied or Thomas Hardy countrified. But provincialism in a critic is a serious fault. A critic has no right to the narrowness which is the frequent prerogative of the creative artist. He has to have a wide outlook or he has not anything at all. Although the novel exercises the rights of a created object, criticism has not those rights, and too many little mansions in English fiction have been acclaimed to their own detriment as important edifices. Take four at random: *Cranford, The Heart of Midlothian, Jane Eyre, Richard Feverel.* For various personal and local reasons we may be attached to these four books. *Cranford* radiates the humour of the urban midlands, *Midlothian* is a handful out of Edinburgh, *Jane Eyre* is the passionate dream of a fine but still undeveloped woman, *Richard Feverel* exudes farmhouse lyricism and flickers with modish wit, but all four are little mansions, not mighty edifices, and we shall see and respect them for what they are if we stand them for an instant in the colonnades of *War and Peace,* or the vaults of *The Brothers Karamazov.*

I shall not often refer to foreign novels in these lectures, still less would I pose as an expert on them who is debarred from discussing them by his terms of reference. But I do want to emphasize their greatness before we start; to cast, so to speak, this preliminary shadow over our subject, so that when we look back on it at the end we may have the better chance of seeing it in its true lights.

So much for the proviso "English." Now for a more important proviso, that of "period or periods." This idea of a period of a development in time, with its consequent emphasis on influences and schools, happens to be exactly what I am hoping to avoid during our brief survey, and I believe that the author of *Gazpacho* will be lenient. Time, all the way through, is to be our enemy. We are to visualize the English novelists not as floating down that stream which bears all its sons away unless they are careful, but as seated together in a room, a circular room, a sort of British Museum reading-room—all writing their novels simultaneously. They do not, as they sit there, think "I live under Queen Victoria, I under Anne, I carry on the tradition of Trollope, I am reacting against Aldous Huxley." The fact that their pens are in their hands is far more vivid to them. They are half mesmerized, their sorrows and joys are pouring out through the ink, they are approximated by the act of creation, and when Professor Oliver Elton says, as he does, that "after 1847 the novel of passion was never to be the same again," none of them understand what he means. That is to be our vision of them—an imperfect vision, but it is suited to our powers, it will preserve us from a serious danger, the danger of pseudo-scholarship.

Genuine scholarship is one of the highest successes which our race can achieve. No one is more triumphant than the man who chooses a worthy subject and masters all its facts and the leading facts of the subjects neighbouring. He can then do what he likes. He can, if his subject is the novel, lecture on it chronologically if he wishes because he has read all the important novels of the past four centuries, many of the unimportant ones, and has adequate knowledge of any collateral facts that bear upon English fiction. The late Sir Walter Raleigh (who once held this lectureship) was such a scholar. Raleigh knew so many facts that he was able to proceed to influences, and his monograph on the English novel adopts the treatment by period which his unworthy successor must avoid. The scholar, like the philosopher, can contemplate the river of time. He contemplates it not as a whole, but he can see the facts, the personalities, floating past him, and estimate the relations between them, and if his conclusions could be as valuable to us as they are to himself he would long ago have civilized the human race. As you know, he has failed. True scholarship is incommunicable, true scholars rare. There are a few scholars, actual or potential, in the audience today, but only a few, and there is certainly none on the platform. Most of us are pseudo-scholars, and I want to consider our characteristics with sympathy and respect, for we are a very large and quite a powerful class, eminent in Church and State, we control the education of the Empire, we lend to the Press such distinction as it consents to receive, and we are a welcome asset at dinner-parties.

Pseudo-scholarship is, on its good side, the homage paid by ignorance to learning. It also has an economic side, on which we need not be hard. Most of us must get a job before thirty, or sponge on our relatives, and many jobs can only be got by passing an exam. The pseudo-scholar often does well in examination (real scholars are not much good), and even when he fails he appreciates their innate majesty. They are gateways to employment, they have power to ban and bless. A paper on *King Lear* may lead somewhere, unlike the rather far-fetched play of the same name. It may be a stepping-stone to the Local Government Board. He does not often put it to himself openly and say "That's the use of knowing things, they help you to get on." The economic pressure he feels is more often subconscious, and he goes to his exam, merely feeling that a paper on *King Lear* is a very tempestuous and terrible experience but an intensely real one. And whether he be cynical or naïf, he is not to be blamed. As long as learning is connected with earning, as long as certain jobs can only be reached through exams, so long must we take the examination system seriously. If another ladder to employment were contrived, much so-called education would disappear, and no one be a penny the stupider.

It is when he comes to criticism—to a job like the present—that he can be so pernicious, because he follows the method of a true scholar without having his equipment. He classes books before he has understood or read them; that is his first crime. Classification by chronology. Books written before 1847, books written after it, books written after or before 1848. The novel in the reign of Queen Anne, the pre-novel, the ur-novel, the novel of the future. Classification by subject matter—sillier still. The literature of Inns, beginning with *Tom Jones;* the literature of the Women's Movement, beginning with *Shirley;*

the literature of Desert Islands, from *Robinson Crusoe* to *The Blue Lagoon;* the literature of Rogues—dreariest of all, though the Open Road runs it pretty close; the literature of Sussex (perhaps the most devoted of the Home Counties); improper books—a serious though dreadful branch of inquiry, only to be pursued by pseudo-scholars of riper years, novels relating to industrialism, aviation, chiropody, the weather. I include the weather on the authority of the most amazing work on the novel that I have met for many years. It came over the Atlantic to me, nor shall I ever forget it. It was a literary manual entitled *Materials and Methods of Fiction.* The writer's name shall be concealed. He was a pseudo-scholar and a good one. He classified novels by their dates, their length, their locality, their sex, their point of view, till no more seemed possible. But he still had the weather up his sleeve, and when he brought it out, it had nine heads. He gave an example under each head, for he was anything but slovenly, and we will run through his list. In the first place the weather can be "decorative," as in Pierre Loti; then "utilitarian," as in *The Mill on the Floss* (no Floss, no Mill; no Mill, no Tullivers); "illustrative," as in *The Egoist;* "planned in pre-established harmony," as by Fiona MacLeod; "in emotional contrast," as in *The Master of Ballantrae;* "determinative of action," as in a certain Kipling story, where a man proposes to the wrong girl on account of a mud storm; "a controlling influence," *Richard Feverel;* "itself a hero," like Vesuvius in

The Last Days of Pompeii; and ninthly, it can be "non-existent," as in a nursery tale. I liked him flinging in nonexistence. It made everything so scientific and trim. But he himself remained a little dissatisfied, and having finished his classification he said yes, of course there was one more thing, and that was genius; it was useless for a novelist to know that there are nine sorts of weather, unless he has genius also. Cheered by this reflection, he classified novels by their tones. There are only two tones, personal and impersonal, and having given examples of each he grew pensive again and said, "Yes, but you must have genius too, or neither tone will profit."

This constant reference to genius is another characteristic of the pseudo-scholar. He loves mentioning genius, because the sound of the word exempts him from trying to discover its meaning. Literature is written by geniuses. Novelists are geniuses. There we are; now let us classify them. Which he does. Everything he says may be accurate but all is useless because he is moving round books instead of through them, he either has not read them or cannot read them properly. Books have to be read (worse luck, for it takes a long time); it is the only way of discovering what they contain. A few savage tribes eat them, but reading is the only method of assimilation revealed to the west. The reader must sit down alone and struggle with the writer, and this the pseudo-scholar will not do. He would rather relate a book to the history of its time, to events in the life of its author, to the events it describes, above all to some tendency. As soon as he can use the word "tendency" his spirits rise, and though those of his audience may sink, they often pull out their pencils at this point and make a note, under the belief that a tendency is portable.

That is why, in the rather ramshackly course that lies ahead of us, we cannot consider fiction by periods, we must not contemplate the stream of time. Another image better suits our powers: that of all the novelists writing their novels at once. They come from different ages and ranks, they have different temperaments and aims, but they all hold pens in their hands, and are in the process of creation. Let us look over their shoulders for a moment and see what they are writing. It may exorcise that demon of chronology which is at present our enemy and which (we shall discover next week) is sometimes their enemy too. "Oh, what quenchless feud is this, that Time hath with the sons of men," cries Herman Melville, and the feud goes on not only in life and death but in the byways of literary creation and criticism. Let us avoid it by imagining that all the novelists are at work together in a circular room. I shall not mention their names until we have heard their words, because a name brings associations with it, dates, gossip, all the furniture of the method we are discarding.

They have been instructed to group themselves in pairs. We approach the first pair, and read as follows:

I. I don't know what to do—not I. God forgive me, but I am very impatient! I wish—but I don't know what to wish without a sin. Yet I wish it would please God to take me to his mercy!—I can meet with none here.—What a world is this!—What is there in it desirable? The good we hope for so strangely mixed, that one knows not what to wish for! And one half of mankind tormenting the other and being tormented themselves in tormenting.

II. What I hate is myself—when I think that one has to take so much, to be happy, out of the lives of others, and that one isn't happy even then. One does it to cheat one's self and to stop one's mouth—but that is only, at the best, for a little. The wretched self is always there, always making us somehow a fresh anxiety. What it comes to is that it's not, that it's never, a happiness, any happiness at all, to *take*. The only safe thing is to give. It's what plays you least false.

It is obvious that here sit two novelists who are looking at life from much the same angle, yet the first of them is Samuel Richardson, and the second you will have already identified as Henry James. Each is an anxious rather than an ardent psychologist. Each is sensitive to suffering and appreciates self-sacrifice; each falls short of the tragic, though a close approach is made. A sort of tremulous nobility—that is the spirit that dominates them—and oh how well they write!—not a word out of place in their copious flows. A hundred and fifty years of time divide them, but are not they close together in other ways, and may not their neighbourliness profit us? Of course as I say this I hear Henry James beginning to express his regret—no, not his regret but his surprise—no, not even his surprise but his awareness that neighbourliness is being postulated of him, and postulated, must he add, in relation to a shopkeeper. And I hear Richardson, equally cautious, wondering whether any writer born outside England can be chaste. But these are surface differences, are indeed no differences at all, but additional points of contact. We leave them sitting in harmony, and proceed to our next pair.

I. All the preparations for the funeral ran easily and happily under Mrs. Johnson's skilful hands. On the eve of the sad occasion she produced a reserve of black sateen, the kitchen steps, and a box of tintacks, and decorated the house with festoons and bows of black in the best possible taste. She tied up the knocker with black crêpe, and put a large bow over the corner of the steel engraving of Garibaldi, and swathed the bust of Mr. Gladstone that had belonged to the deceased with inky swathings. She turned the two vases that had views of Tivoli and the Bay of Naples round, so that these rather brilliant landscapes were hidden and only the plain blue enamel showed, and she anticipated the long contemplated purchase of a tablecloth for the front room, and substituted a violet purple cover for the now very worn and faded raptures and roses in plushette that had hitherto done duty there. Everything that loving consideration could do to impart a dignified solemnity to her little home was done.

II. The air of the parlour being faint with the smell of sweet cake, I looked about for the table of refreshments; it was scarcely visible until one had got accustomed to the gloom, but there was a cut-up plum cake upon it, and there were cut-up oranges, and sandwiches, and biscuits, and two decanters that I knew very well as ornaments, but had never seen used in all my life; one full of port, and one of sherry. Standing at this table, I became conscious of the servile Pumblechook in a black cloak and several yards of hat-band, who was alternately stuffing himself, and making obsequious movements to catch my attention. The moment he succeeded, he came over to me (breathing sherry and crumbs) and said in a subdued voice, "May I, dear sir?" and did.

These two funerals did not by any means happen on the same day. One is the funeral of Mr. Polly's father (1920), the other the funeral of Mrs. Gargery in *Great Expectations* (1860). Yet Wells and Dickens are describing them from the same point of view and even using the same tricks of style (cf. the two vases and the two decanters). They are, both, humorists and visualizers who get an effect by cataloguing details and whisking the page over irritably. They are generous-minded; they hate shams and enjoy being indignant about them; they are valuable social reformers; they have no notion of confining books to a library shelf. Sometimes the lively surface of their prose scratches like a cheap gramophone record, a certain poorness of quality appears, and the face of the author draws rather too near to that of the reader. In other words, neither of them has much taste: the world of beauty was largely closed to Dickens, and is entirely closed to Wells. And there are other parallels—for instance their method of drawing character, but that we shall examine later on. And perhaps the great difference between them is the difference of opportunity offered to an obscure boy of genius a hundred years ago and to a similar boy forty years ago. The difference is all in Wells' favour. He is far better educated than his predecessor; in particular the addition of science has strengthened his mind out of recognition and subdued his hysteria. He registers an improvement in society: Dotheboys Hall has been superseded by the Polytechnic. But he does not register any change in the novelist's art.

What about our next pair?

I. But as for that mark, I'm not sure about it; I don't believe it was made by a nail after all; it's too big, too round, for that I might get up, but if I got up and looked at it, ten to one I shouldn't be able to say for certain; because once a thing's done, no one ever knows how it happened. O dear me, the mystery of life! The inaccuracy of thought! The ignorance of humanity! To show how very little control of our possessions we have—what an accidental affair this living is after all our civilization—let me just count over a few of the things lost on one lifetime, beginning, for that always seems the most mysterious of losses—what cat would gnaw, what rat would nibble—three pale blue canisters of bookbinding tools? Then there were the birdcages, the iron hoops, the steel skates, the Queen Anne coal-scuttle, the bagatelle-board, the hand-organ—all gone, and jewels too. Opals and emeralds, they lie about the roots of turnips. What a scraping paring affair it is to be sure! The wonder is that I've any clothes on my back, that I sit surrounded by solid furniture at this moment. Why, if one wants to compare life to anything one must liken it to being blown through the Tube at fifty miles an hour. . . .

II. Every day for at least ten years together did my father resolve to have it mended; 'tis not mended yet. No family but ours would have borne with it an hour, and what is most astonishing, there was not a subject in the world upon which my father was so eloquent as upon that of door-hinges. And yet, at the same time, he was certainly one of the greatest bubbles to them, I think, that history can produce; his rhetoric and conduct were at perpetual handy-cuffs. Never did the parlour door open but his philosophy or his principles fell a victim to it; three drops of oil with a feather, and a smart stroke of a hammer, had saved his honour for ever.

Inconsistent soul that man is; languishing under wounds which he has the power to heal; his whole life a contradiction to his knowledge; his reason, that precious gift of God to him (instead of pouring in oil), serving but to sharpen his sensibilities, to multiply his pains, and render him more melancholy and uneasy under them! Poor unhappy creature, that he should do so! Are not the necessary causes of misery in this life enough, but he must add voluntary ones to his stock of sorrow? Struggle against evils which cannot be avoided, and submit to others which a tenth part of the trouble they create him would remove from his heart for ever.

By all that is good and virtuous, if there are three drops of oil to be got and a hammer to be found within ten miles of Shandy Hall, the parlour door-hinge shall be mended this reign.

The passage last quoted is, of course, out of *Tristram Shandy*. The other passage was from Virginia Woolf. She and Sterne are both fantasists. They start with a little object, take a flutter from it, and settle on it again. They combine a humorous appreciation of the muddle of life with a keen sense of its beauty. There is even the same tone in their voices—a rather deliberate bewilderment, an announcement to all and sundry that they do not know where they are going. No doubt their scales of value are not the same. Sterne is a sentimentalist, Virginia Woolf (except perhaps in her latest work, *To the Lighthouse*) is extremely aloof. Nor are their achievements on the same scale. But their medium is similar, the same odd effects are obtained by it, the parlour door is never mended, the mark on the wall turns out to be a snail, life is such a muddle, oh, dear, the will is so weak, the sensations fidgety—philosophy—God—oh, dear, look at the mark—listen to the door—existence is really too . . . what were we saying?

Does not chronology seem less important now that we have visualized six novelists at their jobs? If the novel develops, is it not likely to develop on different lines from the British Constitution, or even the Women's Movement? I say "even the Women's Movement" because there happened to be a close association between fiction in England and that movement during the nineteenth century—a connection so close that it has misled some critics into thinking it an organic connection. As women bettered their position, the novel, they asserted, became better too. Quite wrong. A mirror does not develop because an historical pageant passes in front of it. It only develops when it gets a fresh coat of quicksilver—in other words, when it acquires new sensitiveness; and the novel's success lies in its own sensitiveness, not in the success of its subject-matter. Empires fall, votes are accorded, but to those people writing in the circular room it is the feel of the pen between their fingers that matters most. They may decide to write a novel upon the French or the Russian Revolution, but memories, associations, passions, rise up and cloud their objectivity, so that at the close, when they re-read, someone else seems to have been holding their pen and to have relegated their theme to the background. That "someone else" is their self no doubt, but not the self that is so active in time and lives under George IV or V. All through history writers while writing have felt more or less the same. They have entered a common state which it is convenient to call inspiration,[1] and having regard to that state, we may say that History develops, Art stands still.

History develops, Art stands still, is a crude motto, indeed it is almost a slogan, and though forced to adopt it we must not do so without admitting it vulgarily. It contains only a partial truth.

It debars us in the first place from considering whether the human mind alters from generation to generation; whether, for instance, Thomas Deloney, who wrote humorously about shops and pubs in the reign of Queen Elizabeth, differs fundamentally from his modern representative—who would be someone of the calibre of Neil Lyons or Pett Ridge. As a matter of fact Deloney did not differ; differed as an individual, but not fundamentally, not because he lived four hundred years ago. Four thousand, fourteen thousand years might give us pause, but four hundred years is nothing in the life of our race, and does not allow room for any measurable change.

[1] I have touched on this theory of inspiration in a short essay called "Anonymity," Hogarth Press, London.

So our slogan here is no practical hindrance. We can chant it without shame.

It is more serious when we turn to the development of tradition and see what we lose through being debarred from examining that. Apart from schools and influences and fashions, there has been a technique in English fiction, and this does alter from generation to generation. The technique of laughing at characters for instance: to smoke and to rag are not identical; the Elizabethan humorist picks up his victim in a different way from the modern, raises his laugh by other tricks. Or the technique of fantasy: Virginia Woolf, though her aim and general effect both resemble Sterne's, differs from him in execution; she belongs to the same tradition but to a later phase of it. Or the technique of conversation: in my pairs of examples I could not include a couple of dialogues, though I wanted to, for the reason that the use of the "he said" and "she said" varies so much through the centuries that it colours its surroundings, and though the speakers may be similarly conceived they will not seem so in an extract. Well, we cannot examine questions like these, and must admit we are the poorer, though we can abandon the development of subject-matter and the development of the human race without regret. Literary tradition is the borderland lying between literature and history, and the well-equipped critic will spend much time there and enrich his judgment accordingly. We cannot go there because we have not read enough. We must pretend it belongs to history and cut it off accordingly. We must refuse to have anything to do with chronology.

Let me quote here for our comfort from my immediate predecessor in this lectureship, Mr. T. S. Eliot. Mr. Eliot enumerates, in the introduction to *The Sacred Wood,* the duties of the critic. "It is part of his business to preserve tradition—when a good tradition exists. It is part of his business to see literature steadily and to see it whole; and this is eminently to see it *not* as consecrated by time, but to see it beyond time." The first duty we cannot perform, the second we must try to perform. We can neither examine nor preserve tradition. But we can visualize the novelists as sitting in one room, and force them, by our very ignorance, from the limitations of date and place. I think that is worth doing, or I should not have ventured to undertake this course.

How then are we to attack the novel—that spongy tract, those fictions in prose of a certain extent which extend so indeterminately? Not with any elaborate apparatus. Principles and systems may suit other forms of art, but they cannot be applicable here—or if applied their results must be subjected to re-examination. And who is the re-examiner? Well, I am afraid it will be the human heart, it will be this man-to-man business, justly suspect in its cruder forms. The final test of a novel will be our affection for it, as it is the test of our friends, and of anything else which we cannot define. Sentimentality—to some a worse demon than chronology—will lurk in the background saying, "Oh, but I like that," "Oh, but that doesn't appeal to me," and all I can promise is that sentimentality shall not speak too loudly or too soon. The intensely, stifling human quality of the novel is not to be avoided; the novel is sogged with humanity; there is no escaping the uplift or the downpour, nor can they be kept out of criticism. We may hate humanity, but if it is exorcised or even purified the novel wilts; little is left but a bunch of words.

And I have chosen the title "Aspects" because it is unscientific and vague, because it leaves us the maximum of freedom, because it means both the different ways we can look at a novel and the different ways a novelist can look at his work. And the aspects selected for discussion are seven in number: The Story; People; The Plot; Fantasy; Prophecy; Pattern and Rhythm.

Two

THE STORY

WE shall all agree that the fundamental aspect of the novel is its story-telling aspect, but we shall voice our assent in different tones, and it is on the precise tone of voice we employ now that our subsequent conclusions will depend.

Let us listen to three voices. If you ask one type of man, "What does a novel do?" he will reply placidly: "Well—I don't know—it seems a funny sort of question to ask—a novel's a novel—well, I don't know—I suppose it kind of tells a story, so to speak." He is quite good-tempered and vague, and probably driving a motor-bus at the same time and paying no more attention to literature than it merits. Another man, whom I visualize as on a golf-course, will be aggressive and brisk. He will reply: "What does a novel do? Why, tell a story of course, and I've no use for it if it didn't. I like a story. Very bad taste on my part, no doubt, but I like a story. You can take your art, you can take your literature, you can take your music, but give me a good story. And I like a story to be a story, mind, and my wife's the same." And a third man he says in a sort of drooping regretful voice, "Yes—oh, dear, yes—the novel tells a story." I respect and admire the first speaker. I detest and fear the second. And the third is my·self. Yes—oh, dear, yes—the novel tells a story. That is the fundamental aspect without which it could not exist. That is the highest factor common to all novels, and I wish that it was not so, that it could be something different—melody, or perception of the truth, not this low atavistic form.

For the more we look at the story (the story that is a story, mind), the more we disentangle it from the finer growths that it supports, the less shall we find to admire. It runs like a backbone—or may I say a tapeworm, for its beginning and end are arbitrary. It is immensely old—goes back to neolithic times, perhaps to paleolithic. Neanderthal man listened to stories, if one may judge by the shape of his skull. The primitive audience was an audience of shock-heads, gaping round the campfire, fatigued with contending against the mammoth or the woolly rhinoceros, and only kept awake by suspense. What would happen next? The novelist droned on, and as soon as the audience guessed what happened next, they either fell asleep or killed him. We can estimate the dangers incurred when we think of the career of Scheherazade in somewhat later times. Scheherazade avoided her fate because she knew how to wield the weapon of suspense—the only literary tool that has any effect upon tyrants and savages. Great novelist though she was—exquisite in her descriptions, tolerant in her judgments, ingenious in her incidents, advanced in her morality, vivid in her delineations of character, expert in her knowledge of three Oriental capitals—it was yet on none of these gifts that she relied when trying to save her life from her intolerable husband. They were but incidental. She only survived because she managed to keep the king wondering what would happen next. Each time she saw the sun rising she stopped in the middle of a sentence, and left him gaping. "At this moment Scheherazade saw the morning appearing and, discreet, was silent." This uninteresting little phrase is the backbone of the *One Thousand and One Nights,* the tapeworm by which they are tied together and the life of a most accomplished princess was preserved.

We are all like Scheherazade's husband, in that we want to know what happens next. That is universal and that is why the backbone of a novel has to be a story. Some of us want to know nothing else—there is nothing in us but primeval curiosity, and consequently our other literary judgments are ludicrous. And now the story can be defined. It is a narrative of events arranged in their time sequence—dinner coming after breakfast, Tuesday after Monday, decay after death, and so on. *Qua* story, it can only have one merit: that of making the audience want to know what happens next. And conversely it can only have one fault: that of making the audience not want to know what happens next. These are the only two criticisms that can be made on the story that is a story. It is the lowest and simplest of literary organisms. Yet it is the highest factor common to all the very complicated organisms known as novels.

When we isolate the story like this from the nobler aspects through which it moves, and hold it out on the forceps—wriggling and interminable, the naked worm of time—it presents an appearance that is both unlovely and dull. But we have much to learn from it. Let us begin by considering it in connection with daily life.

Daily life is also full of the time-sense. We think one event occurs after or before another, the thought is often in our minds, and much of our talk and action proceeds on the assumption. Much of our talk and action, but not all; there seems something else in life besides time, something which may conveniently be called "value," something which is measured not by minutes or hours, but by intensity, so that when we look at our past it does not stretch back evenly but piles up into a few notable pinnacles, and when we look at the future it seems sometimes a wall, sometimes a cloud, sometimes a sun, but never a chronological chart. Neither memory nor anticipation is much interested in Father Time, and all dreamers, artists and lovers are partially delivered from his tyranny; he can kill them, but he cannot secure their attention, and at the very moment of doom, when the clock collected in the tower its strength and struck, they may be looking the other way. So daily life, whatever it may be really, is practically composed of two lives—the life in time and the life by values—and our conduct reveals a double allegiance. "I only saw her for five minutes, but it was worth it." There you have both allegiances in a single sentence. And what the story does is to narrate the life in time. And what the entire novel does—if it is a good novel—is to include the life by values as well; using devices hereafter to be examined. It, also, pays a double allegiance. But in it, in the novel, the allegiance to time is imperative: no novel could be written without it. Whereas in daily life the allegiance may not be necessary: we do not know, and the experience of certain mystics suggests, indeed, that it is not necessary, and that we are quite mistaken in supposing that Monday is followed by Tuesday, or death by decay. It is always possible for you or me in daily life to deny that time exists and act accordingly even if we become unintelligible and are sent by our fellow citizens to what they choose to call a lunatic asylum. But it is never possible for a novelist to deny time inside the fabric of his novel: he must cling however lightly to the thread of his story, he must touch the interminable tapeworm, otherwise he becomes unintelligible, which, in his case, is a blunder.

I am trying not to be philosophic about time, for it is (experts assure us) a most dangerous hobby for an outsider, far more fatal than place; and quite eminent metaphysicians have been dethroned through referring to it improperly. I am only trying to explain that as I lecture now I hear that clock ticking or do not hear it ticking, I retain or lose the time sense; whereas in a novel there is always a clock.

The author may dislike his clock. Emily Brontë in *Wuthering Heights* tried to hide hers. Sterne, in *Tristram Shandy,* turned his upside down. Marcel Proust, still more ingenious, kept altering the hands, so that his hero was at the same period entertaining a mistress to supper and playing ball with his nurse in the park. All these devices are legitimate, but none of them contravene our thesis: the basis of a novel is a story, and a story is a narrative of events arranged in time sequence. (A story, by the way, is not the same as a plot. It may form the basis of one, but the plot is an organism of a higher type, and will be defined and discussed in a future lecture.)

Who shall tell us a story?

Sir Walter Scott of course.

Scott is a novelist over whom we shall violently divide. For my own part I do not care for him, and find it difficult to understand his continued reputation. His reputation in his day—that is easy to understand. There are important historical reasons for it, which we should discuss if our scheme was chronological. But when we fish him out of the river of time and set him to write in that circular room with the other novelists, he presents a less impressive figure. He is seen to have a trivial mind and a heavy style. He cannot construct. He has neither artistic detachment nor passion, and how can a writer who is devoid of both, create characters who will move us deeply? Artistic detachment—perhaps it is priggish to ask for that. But passion—surely passion is low-brow enough, and think how all Scott's laborious mountains and scooped-out glens and carefully ruined abbeys call out for passion, passion and how it is never there! If he had passion he would be a great writer—no amount of clumsiness or artificiality would matter then. But he only has a temperate heart and gentlemanly feelings, and an intelligent affection for the country-side: and this is not basis enough for great novels. And his integrity—that is worse than nothing, for it was a purely moral and commercial integrity. It satisfied his highest needs and he never dreamt that another sort of loyalty exists.

His fame is due to two causes. In the first place, many of the elder generation had him read aloud to them when they were young; he is entangled with happy sentimental memories, with holidays in or residence in Scotland. They love him indeed for the same reason that I loved and still love *The Swiss Family Robinson.* I could lecture to you now on *The Swiss Family Robinson* and it would be a glowing lecture, because of the emotions felt in boyhood. When my brain decays entirely I shall not bother any more over great literature. I shall go back to the romantic shore where the "ship struck with a fearful shock," emitting four demigods named Fritz, Ernest, Jack and little Franz, together with their father, their mother, and a cushion, which contained all the appliances necessary for a ten years' residence in the tropics. That is my eternal summer, that is what *The Swiss Family Robinson* means to me, and is not it all that Sir Walter Scott means to some of you? Is he really more than a reminder of early happiness? And until our brains do decay, must not we put all this aside when we attempt to understand books?

In the second place, Scott's fame rests upon one genuine basis. He could tell a story. He had the primitive power of keeping the reader in suspense and playing on his curiosity. Let us paraphrase *The Antiquary*—not analyze it, analysis is the wrong method, but paraphrase. Then we shall see the story unrolling itself, and be able to study its simple devices.

THE ANTIQUARY

CHAPTER I

It was early in a fine summer's day, near the end of the eighteenth century, when a young man of genteel appearance, having occasion to go towards the north-east of Scotland, provided himself with a ticket in one of those public carriages which travel between Edinburgh and the Queensferry, at which place, as the name implies, and as is well known to all my northern readers, there is a passage-boat for crossing the Firth of Forth.

That is the first sentence in *The Antiquary*—not an exciting sentence, but it gives us the time, the place, and a young man—it sets the story-teller's scene. We feel a moderate interest in what the young man will do next. His name is Lovel, and there is a mystery about him. He is the hero or Scott would not call him genteel, and he is sure to make the heroine happy. He meets the Antiquary, Jonathan Oldbuck.

They get into the coach, not too quickly, become acquainted, Lovel visits Oldbuck at his house. Near it they meet a new character, Edie Ochiltree. Scott is good at introducing fresh characters. He slides them very naturally, and with a promising air. Edie Ochiltree promises a good deal. He is a beggar—no ordinary beggar, a romantic and reliable rogue, and will he not help to solve the mystery of which we saw the tip in Lovel? More introductions: to Sir Arthur Wardour (old family, bad manager); to his daughter Isabella (haughty), whom the hero loves unrequited; and to Oldbuck's sister Miss Grizzle. Miss Grizzle is introduced with the same air of promise. As a matter of fact she is just a comic turn—she leads nowhere, and your story-teller is full of these turns. He need not hammer away all the time at cause and effect. He keeps just as well within the simple boundaries of his art if he says things that have no bearing on the development. The audience thinks they will develop, but the audience is shock-headed and tired and easily forgets. Unlike the weaver of plots, the story-teller profits by ragged ends. Miss Grizzle is a small example of a ragged end; for a big one I would refer to a novel that professes to be lean and tragic: *The Bride of Lammermoor*. Scott presents the Lord High Keeper in his book with great emphasis and with endless suggestions that the defects of his character will lead to the tragedy, while as a matter of fact the tragedy would occur in almost the same form if he did not exist—the only necessary ingredients in it being Edgar, Lucy, Lady Ashton and

Bucklaw. Well, to return to *The Antiquary,* then there is a dinner, Oldbuck and Sir Arthur quarrel, Sir Arthur is offended and leaves early with his daughter, and they try to walk back to their own house across the sands. Tides rise over sands. The tide rises. Sir Arthur and Isabella are cut off, and are confronted in their peril by Edie Ochiltree. This is the first serious moment in the story and this is how the story-teller who is a story-teller handles it:

While they exchanged these words, they paused upon the highest ledge of rock to which they could attain; for it seemed that any farther attempt to move forward could only serve to anticipate their fate. Here then they were to await the sure, though slow progress of the raging element, something in the situation of the martyrs of the Early Church, who, exposed by heathen tyrants to be slain by wild beasts, were compelled for a time to witness the impatience and rage by which the animals were agitated, while awaiting the signal for undoing their grates and letting them loose upon the victims.

Yet even this fearful pause gave Isabella time to collect the powers of a mind naturally strong and courageous, and which rallied itself at this terrible juncture. "Must we yield life," she said, "without a struggle? Is there no path, however dreadful, by which we could climb the crag, or at least attain some height above the tide, where we could remain till morning, or till help comes? They must be aware of our situation, and will raise the country to relieve us."

Thus speaks the heroine, in accents which certainly chill the reader. Yet we want to know what happens next. The rocks are of cardboard, like those in my dear Swiss Family; the tempest is turned on with one hand while Scott scribbles away about Early Christians with the other; there is no sincerity, no sense of danger in the whole affair; it is all passionless, perfunctory, yet we do just want to know what happens next.

Why—Lovel rescues them. Yes; we ought to have thought of that; and what then?

Another ragged end Lovel is put by the Antiquary to sleep in a haunted room, where he has a dream or vision of his host's ancestor, who says to him, "*Kunst macht Gunst,*" words which he does not understand at the time, owing to his ignorance of German, and learns afterwards that they mean "Skill wins Favour": he must pursue the siege of Isabella's heart. That is to say the supernatural contributes nothing to the story. It is introduced with tapestries and storms, but only a copybook maxim results. The reader does not know this though. When he hears "*Kunst macht Gunst,*" his attention reawakens—then his attention is diverted to something else, and the time-sequence goes on.

Picnic in the ruins of St. Ruth. Introduction of Dousterswivel, a wicked foreigner, who has involved Sir Arthur in mining schemes and whose superstitions are ridiculed because not of the genuine Border band. Arrival of Hector McIntyre, the Antiquary's nephew, who suspects Lovel of being an impostor. The two fight a duel; Lovel, thinking he has killed his opponent, flies with Edie Ochiltree, who has turned up as usual. They hide in the ruins of St. Ruth, where they watch Dousterswivel gulling Sir

Arthur in a treasure-hunt. Lovel gets away on a boat and—out of sight out of mind; we do not worry about him until he turns up again. Second treasure-hunt at St. Ruth. Sir Arthur finds a hoard of silver. Third treasure-hunt. Dousterswivel is soundly cudgelled, and when he comes to himself sees the funeral rites of the old Countess of Glenallan, who is being buried there at midnight and with secrecy, that family being of the Romish persuasion.

Now the Glenallans are very important in the story, yet how casually they are introduced! They are hooked on to Dousterswivel in the most artless way. His pair of eyes happened to be handy, so Scott had a peep through them. And the reader by now is getting so docile under the succession of episodes that he just gapes, like a primitive cave-man. Now the Glenallan interest gets to work, the ruins of St. Ruth are switched off, and we enter what may be called the "pre-story," where two new characters intervene, and talk wildly and darkly about a sinful past. Their names are: Elspeth Mucklebackit, a Sibyl of a fisherwoman, and Lord Glenallan, son of the dead countess. Their dialogue is interrupted by other events—by the arrest, trial and release of Edie Ochiltree, by the death by drowning of another new character, and by the humours of Hector McIntyre's convalescence at his uncle's house. But the gist is that Lord Glenallan many years ago had married a lady called Evelina Nevile, against his mother's wish, and had then been given to understand that she was his half-sister. Maddened with horror, he had left her before she gave birth to a child. Elspeth, formerly his mother's servant, now explains to him that Evelina was no relation to him, that she died in childbirth—Elspeth and another woman attending—and that the child disappeared. Lord Glenallan then goes to consult the Antiquary, who, as a Justice of the Peace, knew something of the events of the time, and who had also loved Evelina. And what happens next? Sir Arthur Wardour's goods are sold up, for Dousterswivel has ruined him. And then? The French are reported to be landing. And then? Lovel rides into the district leading the British troops. He calls himself "Major Nevile" now. But even "Major Nevile" is not his right name, for he is who but the lost child of Lord Glenallan, he is none other than the legitimate heir to an earldom. Partly through Elspeth Mucklebackit, partly through her fellow servant whom he meets as a nun abroad, partly through an uncle who has died, partly through Edie Ochiltree, the truth has come out. There are indeed plenty of reasons for the *dénouement,* but Scott is not interested in reasons; he dumps them down without bothering to elucidate them; to make one thing happen after another is his only serious aim. And then? Isabella Wardour relents and marries the hero. And then? That is the end of the story. We must not ask "And then?" too often. If the time-sequence is pursued one second too far it leads us into quite another country.

The Antiquary is a book in which the life in time is celebrated instinctively by the novelist, and this must lead to slackening of emotion and shallowness of judgment, and in particular to that idiotic use of marriage as a finale. Time can be celebrated consciously also, and we shall find an example of this in a very different sort of book, a memorable book: Arnold Bennett's *The Old Wives' Tale.* Time is the real hero of *The Old Wives' Tale.* He is installed as the lord of creation—excepting indeed of Mr. Critchlow, whose bizarre exemption only gives added force. Sophia and Constance are the children of Time from the instant we see them romping with their mother's dresses; they are doomed to decay with a completeness that is very rare in literature. They are girls, Sophia runs away and marries, the mother dies, Constance marries, her husband dies, Sophia's husband dies, Sophia dies, Constance dies, their old rheumatic dog lumbers up to see whether anything remains in the saucer. Our daily life in time is exactly this business of getting old which clogs the arteries of Sophia and Constance, and the story that is a story and sounded so healthy and stood no nonsense cannot sincerely lead to any conclusion but the grave. It is an unsatisfactory conclusion. Of course we grow old. But a great book must rest on something more than an "of course," and *The Old Wives' Tale* is very strong, sincere and sad—it misses greatness.

What about *War and Peace*? That is certainly great, that likewise emphasizes the effects of time and the waxing and waning of a generation. Tolstoy, like Bennett, has the courage to show us people getting old—the partial decay of Nicolay and Natasha is really more sinister than the complete decay of Constance and Sophia: more of our own youth seems to have perished in it. Then why is *War and Peace* not depressing? Probably because it has extended over space as well as over time, and the sense of space until it terrifies us is exhilarating, and leaves behind it an effect like music. After one has read *War and Peace* for a bit, great chords begin to sound, and we cannot say exactly what struck them. They do not arise from the story, though Tolstoy is quite as interested in what comes next as Scott, and quite as sincere as Bennett. They do not come from the episodes nor yet from the characters. They come from the immense area of Russia, over which episodes and characters have been scattered, from the sum-total of bridges and frozen rivers, forests, roads, gardens, fields, which accumulate grandeur and sonority after we have passed them. Many novelists have the feeling for place—Five Towns, Auld Reekie, and so on. Very few have the sense of space, and the possession of it ranks high in Tolstoy's divine equipment. Space is the lord of *War and Peace,* not time.

A word in conclusion about the story as the repository of a voice. It is the aspect of the novelist's work which asks to be read out loud, which appeals not to the eye, like most prose, but to the ear; having indeed this much in common with oratory. It does not offer melody or cadence. For these, strange as it may seem, the eye is sufficient; the eye, backed by a mind that transmutes, can easily gather up the sounds of a paragraph or dialogue when they have aesthetic value, and refer them to our enjoyment—yes, can even telescope them up so that we get them quicker than we should do if they were recited, just as some people can look through a musical score quicker than it can be rapped out on the piano. But the eye is not equally quick at catching a voice. That opening sentence of *The Antiquary* has no beauty of sound, yet we should lose something if it was not read aloud. Our mind would commune with Walter Scott's silently, and less profitably. The story, besides saying one thing after another, adds something because of its connection with a voice.

It does not add much. It does not give us anything as important as the author's personality. His personality—when he has one—is conveyed through nobler agencies, such as the characters or the plot or his comments on life. What the story does do in this particular capacity, all it can do, is to transform us from readers into listeners, to whom "a" voice speaks, the voice of the tribal narrator, squatting in the middle of the cave, and saying one thing after another until the audience falls asleep among their offal and bones. The story is primitive, it reaches back to the origins of literature, before reading was discovered, and it appeals to what is primitive in us. That is why we are so unreasonable over the stories we like, and so ready to bully those who like something else. For instance, I am annoyed when people laugh at me for loving *The Swiss Family Robinson,* and I hope that I have annoyed some of you over Scott! You see what I mean. Intolerance is the atmosphere stories generate. The story is neither moral nor is it favourable to the understanding of the novel in its other aspects. If we want to do that we must come out of the cave.

We shall not come out of it yet, but observe already how that other life—the life by value—presses against the novel from all sides, how it is ready to fill and indeed distort it, offering it people, plots, fantasies, views of the universe, anything except this constant "and then . . . and then," which is the sole contribution of our present inquiry. The life in time is so obviously base and inferior that the question naturally occurs: cannot the novelist abolish it from his work, even as the mystic asserts he has abolished it from his experience, and install its radiant alternative alone?

Well, there is one novelist who has tried to abolish time, and her failure is instructive: Gertrude Stein. Going much further than Emily Brontë, Sterne or Proust, Gertrude Stein has smashed up and pulverized her clock and scattered its fragments over the world like the limbs of Osiris, and she has done this not from naughtiness but from a noble motive: she has hoped to emancipate fiction from the tyranny of time and to express in it the life by values only. She fails, because as soon as fiction is completely delivered from time it cannot express anything at all, and in her later writing we can see the slope down which she is slipping. She wants to abolish this whole aspect of the story, this sequence in chronology, and my heart goes out to her. She cannot do it without abolishing the sequence between the sentences. But this is not effective unless the order of the words in the sentences is also abolished, which in its turn entails the abolition of the order of the letters or sounds in the words. And now she is over the precipice. There is nothing to ridicule in such an experiment as hers. It is much more important to play about like this than to rewrite the Waverley Novels. Yet the experiment is doomed to failure. The time-sequence cannot be destroyed without carrying in its ruin all that should have taken its place; the novel that would express values only becomes unintelligible and therefore valueless.

That is why I must ask you to join me in repeating in exactly the right tone of voice the words with which this lecture opened. Do not say them vaguely and good-temperedly like a busman: you have not the right. Do not say them briskly and aggressively like a golfer: you know better. Say them a little sadly, and you will be correct. Yes—oh, dear, yes—the novel tells a story.

Three

PEOPLE

HAVING discussed the story—that simple and fundamental aspect of the novel—we can turn to a more interesting topic: the actors. We need not ask what happened next, but to whom did it happen; the novelist will be appealing to our intelligence and imagination, not merely to our curiosity. A new emphasis enters his voice: emphasis upon value.

Since the actors in a story are usually human, it seemed convenient to entitle this aspect People. Other animals have been introduced, but with limited success, for we know too little so far about their psychology. There may be, probably will be, an alteration here in the future, comparable to the alteration in the novelist's rendering of savages in the past. The gulf that separates Man Friday from Batouala may be paralleled by the gulf that will separate Kipling's wolves from their literary descendants two hundred years hence, and we shall have animals who are neither symbolic, nor little men disguised, nor as four-legged tables moving, nor as painted scraps of paper that fly. It is one of the ways where science may enlarge the novel, by giving it fresh subject-matter. But the help has not been given yet, and until it comes we may say that the actors in a story are, or pretend to be, human beings.

Since the novelist is himself a human being, there is an affinity between him and his subject-matter which is absent in many other forms of art. The historian is also linked, though, as we shall see, less intimately. The painter and sculptor need not be linked: that is to say they need not represent human beings unless they wish, no more need the poet, while the musician cannot represent them even if he wishes, without the help of a programme. The novelist, unlike many of his colleagues, makes up a number of word-masses roughly describing himself (roughly: niceties shall come later), gives them names and sex, assigns them plausible gestures, and causes them to speak by the use of inverted commas, and perhap to behave consistently. These word-masses are his characters. They do not come thus coldly to his mind, they may be created in delirious excitement; still, their nature is conditioned by what he guesses about other people, and about himself, and is further modified by the other aspects of his work. This last point—the relation of characters to the other aspects of the novel—will form the subject of a future inquiry. At present we are occupied with their relation to actual life. What is the difference between people in a novel and people like the novelist or like you, or like me, or Queen Victoria?

There is bound to be a difference. If a character in a novel is exactly like Queen Victoria—not rather like but exactly like—then it actually is Queen Victoria, and the novel, or all of it that the character touches, becomes a memoir. A memoir is history, it is based on evidence. A novel is based on evidence + or − *x*, the unknown quantity being the temperament of the novelist, and the unknown quantity always modifies the effect of the evidence, and sometimes transforms it entirely.

The historian deals with actions, and with the characters of men only so far as he can deduce them from their actions. He is quite as much concerned with character as the novelist, but he can only know of its existence when it shows on the surface. If Queen Victoria had not said, "We are not amused," her neighbours at table would not have known she was not amused, and her ennui could never have been announced to the public. She might have frowned, so that they would have deduced her state from that—looks and gestures are also historical evidence. But if she remained impassive—what would anyone know? The hidden life is, by definition, hidden. The hidden life that appears in external signs is hidden no longer, has entered the realm of action. And it is the function of the novelist to reveal the hidden life at its source: to tell us more about Queen Victoria than could be known, and thus to produce a character who is not the Queen Victoria of history.

The interesting and sensitive French critic who writes under the name of Alain has some helpful if slightly fantastic remarks on this point. He gets a little out of his depth, but not as much as I feel myself out of mine, and perhaps together we may move toward the shore. Alain examines in turn the various forms of aesthetic activity, and coming in time to the novel (*le roman*) he asserts that each human being has two sides, appropriate to history and fiction. All that is observable in a man—that is to say his actions and such of his spiritual existence as can be deduced from his actions—falls into the domain of history. But his romanceful or romantic side (*sa partie romanesque ou romantique*) includes "the pure passions, that is to say the dreams, joys, sorrows and self-communings which politeness or shame prevent him from mentioning"; and to express this side of human nature is one of the chief functions of the novel. "What is fictitious in a novel is not so much the story as the method by which thought develops into action, a method which never occurs in daily life. . . . History, with its emphasis on external causes, is dominated by the notion of fatality, whereas there is no fatality in the novel; there, everything is founded on human nature, and the dominating feeling is of an existence where everything is intentional, even passions and crimes, even misery." [1]

This is perhaps a roundabout way of saying what every British schoolboy knew, that the historian records whereas the novelist must create. Still, it is a profitable roundabout, for it brings out the funda-

[1] Paraphrased from *Système des Beaux Arts*, pp. 314-315. I am indebted to M. André Maurois for introducing me to this stimulating essay.

mental difference between people in daily life and people in books. In daily life we never understand each other, neither complete clairvoyance nor complete confessional exists. We know each other approximately, by external signs, and these serve well enough as a basis for society and even for intimacy. But people in a novel can be understood completely by the reader, if the novelist wishes; their inner as well as their outer life can be exposed. And this is why they often seem more definite than characters in history, or even our own friends; we have been told all about them that can be told; even if they are imperfect or unreal they do not contain any secrets, whereas our friends do and must, mutual secrecy being one of the conditions of life upon this globe.

Now let us restate the problem in a more schoolboyish way. You and I are people. Had not we better glance through the main facts in our own lives—not in our individual careers but in our make-up as human beings? Then we shall have something definite to start from.

The main facts in human life are five: birth, food, sleep, love and death. One could increase the number—add breathing for instance—but these five are the most obvious. Let us briefly ask ourselves what part they play in our lives, and what in novels. Does the novelist tend to reproduce them accurately or does he tend to exaggerate, minimize, ignore, and to exhibit his characters going through processes which are not the same through which you and I go, though they bear the same names?

To consider the two strangest first: birth and death; strange because they are at the same time experiences and not experiences. We only know of them by report. We were all born, but we cannot remember what it was like. And death is coming even as birth has come, but, similarly, we do not know what it is like. Our final experience, like our first, is conjectural. We move between two darknesses. Certain people pretend to tell us what birth and death are like: a mother, for instance, has her point of view about birth; a doctor, a religious, have their points of view about both. But it is all from the outside, and the two entities who might enlighten us, the baby and the corpse, cannot do so, because their apparatus for communicating their experiences is not attuned to our apparatus for reception.

So let us think of people as starting life with an experience they forget and ending it with one which they anticipate but cannot understand. These are the creatures whom the novelist proposes to introduce as characters into books; these, or creatures plausibly like them. The novelist is allowed to remember and understand everything, if it suits him. He knows all the hidden life. How soon will he pick up his characters after birth, how close to the grave will he follow them? And what will he say, or cause to be felt, about these two queer experiences?

Then food, the stoking-up process, the keeping alive of an individual flame, the process that begins before birth and is continued after it by the mother, and finally taken over by the individual himself, who goes on day after day putting an assortment of objects into a hole in his face without becoming surprised or bored: food is a link between the known and the forgotten; closely connected with birth, which none of us remembers, and coming down to this morning's breakfast. Like sleep—which in many ways it resembles—food does not merely restore our strength, it has also an aesthetic side, it can taste good or bad. What will happen to this double-faced commodity in books?

And fourthly, sleep. On the average, about a third of our time is not spent in society or civilization or even in what is usually called solitude. We enter a world of which little is known and which seems to us after leaving it to have been partly oblivion, partly a caricature of this world and partly a revelation. "I dreamt of nothing" or "I dreamt of a ladder" or "I dreamt of heaven" we say when we wake. I do not want to discuss the nature of sleep and dreams—only to point out that they occupy much time and that what is called "History" only busies itself with about two-thirds of the human cycle, and theorizes accordingly. Does fiction take up a similar attitude?

And lastly, love. I am using this celebrated word in its widest and dullest sense. Let me be very dry and brief about sex in the first place. Some years after a human being is born, certain changes occur in it, as in other animals, which changes often lead to union with another human being, and to the production of more human beings. And our race goes on. Sex begins before adolescence, and survives sterility; it is indeed coeval with our lives, although at the mating age its effects are more obvious to society. And besides sex, there are other emotions, also strengthening towards maturity: the various upliftings of the spirit, such as affection, friendship, patriotism, mysticism—and as soon as we try to determine the relation between sex and these other emotions we shall of course begin to quarrel as violently as we ever could about Walter Scott, perhaps even more violently. Let me only tabulate the various points of view. Some people say that sex is basic and underlies all these other loves—love of friends, of God, of country. Others say that it is connected with them, but laterally; it is not their root. Others say that it is not connected at all. All I suggest is that we call the whole bundle of emotions love, and regard them as the fifth great experience through which human beings have to pass. When human beings love they try to get something. They also try to give something, and this double aim makes love more complicated than food or sleep. It is selfish and altruistic at the same time, and no amount of specialization in one direction quite atrophies the other. How much time does love take? This question sounds gross but it must be asked because it bears on our present inquiry. Sleep takes about eight hours out of the twenty-four, food about two more. Shall we put down love for another two? Surely that is a handsome allowance. Love may weave itself into our other activities—so may drowsiness and hunger. Love may start various secondary activities: for instance, a man's love for his family may cause him to spend a good deal of time on the Stock Exchange, or his love for God a good deal of time in church. But that he has emotional communion with any beloved object for more than two hours a day may be gravely doubted, and it is this emotional communion, this desire to give and to get, this mixture of generosity and expectation, that distinguishes love from the other experiences on our list.

That is the human make-up—or part of it. Made up like this himself, the novelist takes his pen in his hand, gets into the abnormal state which it is convenient to call "inspiration," and tries to create characters. Perhaps the characters have to fall in with something else in his novel: this often happens (the books of Henry James are an extreme case), and then the characters have, of course, to modify the make-up accordingly. However, we are considering now the more simple case of the novelist whose main passion is human beings and who will sacrifice a great deal to their convenience—story, plot, form, incidental beauty.

Well, in what senses do the nations of fiction differ from those of the earth? One cannot generalize about them, because they have nothing in common in the scientific sense; they need not have glands, for example, whereas all human beings have glands. Nevertheless, though incapable of strict definition, they tend to behave along the same lines.

In the first place, they come into the world more like parcels than human beings. When a baby arrives in a novel it usually has the air of having been posted. It is delivered "off"; one of the elder characters goes and picks it up and shows it to the reader, after which it is usually laid in cold storage until it can talk or otherwise assist in the action. There is both a good and bad reason for this and for all other deviations from earthly practice; these we will note in a minute, but do just observe in what a very perfunctory way the population of noveldom is recruited. Between Sterne and James Joyce, scarcely any writer has tried either to use the facts of birth or to invent a new set of facts, and no one, except in a sort of auntish wistful way, has tried to work back towards the psychology of the baby's mind and to utilize the literary wealth that must lie there. Perhaps it cannot be done. We shall decide in a moment.

Death. The treatment of death, on the other hand, is nourished much more on observation, and has a variety about it which suggests that the novelist finds it congenial. He does, for the reason that death ends a book neatly, and for the less obvious reason that working as he does in time he finds it easier to work from the known towards the darkness rather than from the darkness of birth towards the known. By the time his characters die, he understands them; he can be both appropriate and imaginative about them—strongest of combinations. Take a little death —the death of Mrs. Proudie in the *Last Chronicle of Barset.* All is in keeping, yet the effect is terrifying, because Trollope has ambled Mrs. Proudie down many a diocesan bypath, showing her paces, making her snap, accustoming us, even to boredom, to her character and tricks, to her "Bishop, consider the souls of the people," and then she has a heart attack by the edge of her bed, she has ambled far enough—end of Mrs. Proudie. There is scarcely anything that the novelist cannot borrow from "daily death"; scarcely anything he may not profitably invent. The doors of that darkness lie open to him and he can even follow his characters through it, provided he is shod with imagination and does not try to bring us back scraps of séance information about the "life beyond."

What of food, the third fact upon our list? Food in fiction is mainly social. It draws characters together, but they seldom require it physiologically, seldom enjoy it, and never digest it unless specially asked to do so. They hunger for each other, as we do in life, but our equally constant longing for breakfast and lunch does not get reflected. Even poetry has made more of it—at least of its aesthetic side. Milton and Keats have both come nearer to the sensuousness of swallowing than George Meredith.

Sleep. Also perfunctory. No attempt to indicate oblivion or the actual dream world. Dreams are either logical or else mosaics made out of hard little fragments of the past and future. They are introduced with a purpose and that purpose is not the character's life as a whole, but that part of it he lives while awake. He is never conceived as a creature, a third of whose time is spent in the darkness. It is the limited daylight vision of the historian, which the novelist elsewhere avoids. Why should he not understand or reconstruct sleep? For remember, he has the right to invent, and we know when he is inventing truly, because his passion floats us over improbabilities. Yet he has neither copied sleep nor created it. It is just an amalgam.

Love. You all know how enormously love bulks in novels, and will probably agree with me that it has done them harm and made them monotonous. Why has this particular experience, especially in its sex form, been transplanted in such generous quantities? If you think of a novel in the vague you think of a love interest—of a man and woman who want to be united and perhaps succeed. If you think of your own life in the vague, or of a group of lives, you are left with a very different and a more complex impression.

There would seem to be two reasons why love, even in good sincere novels, is unduly prominent.

Firstly, when the novelist ceases to design his characters and begins to create them—"love" in any or all of its aspects becomes important in his mind, and without intending to do so he makes his characters unduly sensitive to it—unduly in the sense that they would not trouble so much in life. The constant sensitiveness of characters for each other—even in writers called robust, like Fielding—is remarkable, and has no parallel in life, except among people who have plenty of leisure. Passion, intensity at moments—yes, but not this constant awareness, this endless readjusting, this ceaseless hunger. I believe that these are the reflections of the novelist's own state of mind while he composes, and that the predominance of love in novels is partly because of this.

A second reason; which logically comes into another part of our inquiry, but it shall be noted here. Love, like death, is congenial to a novelist because it ends a book conveniently. He can make it a permanency, and his readers easily acquiesce, because one of the illusions attached to love is that it will be permanent. Not has been—will be. All history, all our experience, teaches us that no human relationship is constant, it is as unstable as the living beings who compose it, and they must balance like jugglers if it is to remain; if it is constant it is no longer a human relationship but a social habit, the emphasis in it has passed from love to marriage. All this we know, yet we cannot bear to apply our bitter knowledge to the future; the future is to be so different; the perfect person is to come along, or the person we know already is to become perfect. There are to be no changes, no necessity for alertness. We are to be happy or even perhaps miserable for ever and ever. Any strong emotion brings with it the illusion of permanence, and the novelists have seized upon this. They usually end their books with marriage, and we do not object because we lend them our dreams.

Here we must conclude our comparison of those two allied species, *homo sapiens* and *homo fictus*. *Homo fictus* is more elusive than his cousin. He is created in the minds of hundreds of different novelists, who have conflicting methods of gestation, so one must not generalize. Still, one can say a little about him. He is generally born off, he is capable of dying on, he wants little food or sleep, he is tirelessly occupied with human relationships. And—most important—we can know more about him than we can know about any of our fellow creatures, because his creator and narrator are one. Were we equipped for hyperbole we might exclaim at this point: "If God could tell the story of the Universe, the Universe would become fictitious."

For this is the principle involved.

Let us, after these high speculations, take an easy character and study it for a little. Moll Flanders will do. She fills the book that bears her name, or rather stands alone in it, like a tree in a park, so that we can see her from every aspect and are not bothered by rival growths. Defoe is telling a story, like Scott, and we shall find stray threads left about in much the same way, on the chance of the writer wanting to pick them up afterwards: Moll's early batch of children for instance. But the parallel between Scott and Defoe cannot be pressed. What interested Defoe was the heroine, and the form of his book proceeds naturally out of her character. Seduced by a younger brother and married to an elder, she takes to husbands in the earlier and brighter part of her career: not to prostitution, which she detests with all the force of a decent and affectionate heart. She and most of the characters in Defoe's underworld are kind to one another, they save each other's feelings and run risks through personal loyalty. Their innate goodness is always flourishing despite the author's better judgment, the reason evidently being that the author had some great experience himself while in Newgate. We do not know what it was, probably he himself did not know afterwards, for he was a busy slipshod journalist and a keen politician. But something occurred to him in prison, and out of its vague, powerful emotion Moll and Roxana are born. Moll is a character physically, with hard plump limbs that get into bed and pick pockets. She lays no stress upon her appearance, yet she moves us as having height and weight, as breathing and eating, and doing many of the things that are usually missed out. Husbands were her earlier employ: she was trigamous if not quadrigamous, and one of her husbands turned out to be a brother. She was happy with all of them, they were nice to her, she nice to them. Listen to the pleasant jaunt her draper husband took her on—she never cared for him much.

> "Come, my dear," says he to me one day, "shall we go and take a turn into the country for about a week?" "Ay, my dear," says I, "whither would you go?" "I care not whither," says he, "but I have a mind to look like quality for a week. We'll go to Oxford," says he. "How," says I, "shall we go? I am no horse-woman, and 'tis too far for a coach." "Too far!" says he; "no place is too far for a coach-and-six. If I carry you out, you shall travel like a duchess." "Hum," says I, "my dear, 'tis a frolic; but it you have a mind to it, I don't care." Well, the time

was appointed, we had a rich coach, very good horses, a coachman, postilion, and two footmen in very good liveries; a gentleman on horseback, and a page with a feather in his hat upon another horse. The servants all called my lord, and the inn-keepers, you may be sure, did the like, and I was her honour the Countess, and thus we travelled to Oxford, and a very pleasant journey we had; for, give him his due, not a beggar alive knew better how to be a lord than my husband. We saw all the rarities at Oxford, talked with two or three Fellows of Colleges about putting out a young nephew, that was left to his lordship's care, to the University, and of their being his tutors. We diverted ourselves with bantering several other poor scholars, with hopes of being at least his lordship's chaplains, and putting on a scarf; and thus having lived like quality, indeed, as to expense, we went away for Northampton, and, in a word, in about twelve days' ramble came home again, to the tune of about £93 expense.

Contrast with this the scene with her Lancashire husband, whom she deeply loved. He is a highwayman, and each by pretending to wealth has trapped the other into marriage. After the ceremony, they are mutually unmasked, and if Defoe were writing mechanically he would set them to upbraid one another, like Mr. and Mrs. Lammle in *Our Mutual Friend*. But he has given himself over to the humour and good sense of his heroine. She guides him through.

"Truly," said I to him, "I found you would soon have conquered me; and it is my affliction now, that I am not in a condition to let you see how easily I should have been reconciled to you, and have passed by all the tricks you had put upon me, in recompense of so much good-humour. But, my dear," said I, "what can we do now? We are both undone, and what better are we for our being reconciled together, seeing we have nothing to live on?"

We proposed a great many things, but nothing could offer where there was nothing to begin with. He begged me at last to talk no more of it, for, he said, I would break his heart; so we talked of other things a little, till at last he took a husband's leave of me, and so we went to sleep.

Which is both truer to daily life and pleasanter to read than Dickens. The couple are up against facts, not against the author's theory of morality, and being sensible good-hearted rogues, they do not make a fuss. In the later part of her career she turns from husbands to thieving; she thinks this a change for the worse and a natural darkness spreads over the scene. But she is as firm and amusing as ever. How just are her reflections when she robs of her gold necklace the little girl returning from the dancing-class. The deed is done in the little passage leading to St. Bartholomew's, Smithfield (you can visit the place today—Defoe haunts London) and her impulse is to kill the child as well. She does not, the impulse is very feeble, but conscious of the risk the child has run she becomes most indignant with the parents for "leaving the poor little lamb to come home by itself, and it would teach them to take more care of it another time." How heavily and pretentiously a modern psychologist would labour to express this! It just runs off Defoe's pen, and so in another passage, where Moll cheats a man, and then tells him pleasantly afterwards that she has done so, with the result that she slides still further into his good graces, and cannot bear to cheat him any more. Whatever she does gives us a slight shock—not the jolt of disillusionment, but the thrill that proceeds from a living being. We laugh at her, but without bitterness or superiority. She is neither hypocrite nor fool.

Towards the end of the book she is caught in a draper's shop by two young ladies from behind the counter: "I would have given them good words but there was no room for it: two fiery dragons could not have been more furious than they were"—they call for the police, she is arrested and sentenced to death and then transported to Virginia instead. The clouds of misfortune lift with indecent rapidity. The voyage is a very pleasant one, owing to the kindness of the old woman who had originally taught her to steal. And (better still) her Lancashire husband happens to be transported also. They land at Virginia where, much to her distress, her brother-husband proves to be in residence. She conceals this, he dies, and the Lancashire husband only blames her for concealing it from him: he has no other grievance, for the reason that he and she are still in love. So the book closes prosperously, and firm as at the opening sentence the heroine's voice rings out: "We resolve to spend the remainder of our years in sincere penitence for the wicked lives we have led."

Her penitence is sincere, and only a superficial judge will condemn her as a hypocrite. A nature such as hers cannot for long distinguish between doing wrong and getting caught—for a sentence or two she disentangles them but they insist on blending, and that is why her outlook is so cockneyfied and natural, with "sich is life" for a philosophy and Newgate in the place of Hell. If we were to press her or her creator Defoe and say, "Come, be serious. Do you believe in Infinity?" they would say (in the parlance of their modern descendants), "Of course I believe in Infinity—what do you take me for?"—a confession of faith that slams the door on Infinity more completely than could any denial.

Moll Flanders then shall stand as our example of a novel in which a character is everything and is given freest play. Defoe makes a slight attempt at a plot with the brother-husband as a centre, but he is quite perfunctory, and her legal husband (the one who took her on the jaunt to Oxford) just disappears and is heard of no more. Nothing matters but the heroine; she stands in an open space like a tree, and having said that she seems absolutely real from every point of view, we must ask ourselves whether we should recognize her if we met her in daily life. For that is the point we are still considering: the difference between people in life and people in books. And the odd thing is, that even though we take a character as natural and untheoretical as Moll who would coincide with daily life in every detail, we should not find her there as a whole. Suppose I suddenly altered my voice from a lecturing voice into an ordinary one and said to you, "Look out—I can see Moll in the audience—look out, Mr."—naming one of you by name—"she as near as could be got your watch"—well, you would know at once that I was wrong, that I was sinning not only against probabilities, which does not signify, but against daily life and books and the gulf that divides them. If I said, "Look out, there's someone like Moll in the audience," you might not believe me but you would not be annoyed by my imbecile lack of taste: I should only be sinning against probability. To suggest that Moll is in Cambridge this afternoon or anywhere in England, or has been anywhere in England is idiotic. Why?

This particular question will be easy to answer next week, when we shall deal with more complicated novels, where the character has to fit in with other aspects of fiction. We shall then be able to make the usual reply, which we find in all manuals of literature, and which should always be given in an examination paper, the aesthetic reply, to the effect that a novel is a work of art, with its own laws, which are not those of daily life, and that a character in a novel is real when it lives in accordance with such laws. Amelia or Emma, we shall then say, cannot be at this lecture because they exist only in the books called after them, only in worlds of Fielding or Jane Austen. The barrier of art divides them from us. They are real not because they are like ourselves (though they may be like us) but because they are convincing.

It is a good answer, it will lead on to some sound

conclusions. Yet it is not satisfactory for a novel like *Moll Flanders,* where the character is everything and can do what it likes. We want a reply that is less aesthetic and more psychological. Why cannot she be here? What separates her from us? Our answer has already been implied in that quotation from Alain: she cannot be here because she belongs to a world where the secret life is visible, to a world that is not and cannot be ours, to a world where the narrator and the creator are one. And now we can get a definition as to when a character in a book is real: it is real when the novelist knows everything about it. He may not choose to tell us all he knows—many of the facts, even of the kind we call obvious, may be hidden. But he will give us the feeling that though the character has not been explained, it is explicable, and we get from this a reality of a kind we can never get in daily life.

For human intercourse, as soon as we look at it for its own sake and not as a social adjunct, is seen to be haunted by a spectre. We cannot understand each other, except in a rough and ready way; we cannot reveal ourselves, even when we want to; what we call intimacy is only a makeshift; perfect knowledge is an illusion. But in the novel we can know people perfectly, and, apart from the general pleasure of reading, we can find here a compensation for their dimness in life. In this direction fiction is truer than history, because it goes beyond the evidence, and each of us knows from his own experience that there is something beyond the evidence, and even if the novelist has not got it correctly, well—he has tried. He can post his people in as babies, he can cause them to go on without sleep or food, he can make them be in love, love and nothing but love, provided he seems to know everything about them, provided they are his creations. That is why Moll Flanders cannot be here, that is one of the reasons why Amelia and Emma cannot be here. They are people whose secret lives are visible or might be visible: we are people whose secret lives are invisible.

And that is why novels, even when they are about wicked people, can solace us; they suggest a more comprehensible and thus a more manageable human race, they give us the illusion of perspicacity and of power.

Four

PEOPLE (*Continued*)

WE now turn from transplantation to acclimatization. We have discussed whether people could be taken out of life and put into a book, and conversely whether they could come out of books and sit down in this room. The answer suggested was in the negative and led to a more vital question: can we, in daily life, understand each other? Today our problems are more academic. We are concerned with the characters in their relation to other aspects of the novel; to a plot, a moral, their fellow characters, atmosphere, etc. They will have to adapt themselves to other requirements of their creator.

It follows that we shall no longer expect them to coincide as a whole with daily life, only to parallel it. When we say that a character in Jane Austen, Miss Bates for instance, is "so like life" we mean that each bit of her coincides with a bit of life, but that she as a whole only parallels the chatty spinster we met at tea. Miss Bates is bound by a hundred threads to Highbury. We cannot tear her away without bringing her mother too, and Jane Fairfax and Frank Churchill, and the whole of Box

Hill; whereas we could tear Moll Flanders away, at least for the purposes of experiment. A Jane Austen novel is more complicated than a Defoe, because the characters are inter-dependent, and there is the additional complication of a plot. The plot in *Emma* is not prominent and Miss Bates contributes little. Still it is there, she is connected with the principals, and the result is a closely woven fabric from which nothing can be removed. Miss Bates and Emma herself are like bushes in a shrubbery—not isolated trees like Moll—and anyone who has tried to thin out a shrubbery knows how wretched the bushes look if they are transplanted elsewhere, and how wretched is the look of the bushes that remain. In most books the characters cannot spread themselves. They must exercise a mutual restraint.

The novelist, we are beginning to see, has a very mixed lot of ingredients to handle. There is the story, with its time-sequence of "and then . . . and then . . ."; there are ninepins about whom he might tell the story, and tell a rattling good one, but no, he prefers to tell his story about human beings; he takes over the life by values as well as the life in time. The characters arrive when evoked, but full of the spirit of mutiny. For they have these numerous parallels with people like ourselves, they try to live their own lives and are consequently often engaged in treason against the main scheme of the book. They "run away," they "get out of hand": they are creations inside a creation, and often inharmonious towards it; if they are given complete freedom they kick the book to pieces, and if they are kept too sternly in check, they revenge themselves by dying, and destroy it by intestinal decay.

These trials beset the dramatist also, and he has yet another set of ingredients to cope with—the actors and actresses—and they appear to side sometimes with the characters they represent, sometimes with the play as a whole, and more often to be the mortal enemies of both. The weight they throw is incalculable, and how any work of art survives their arrival I do not understand. Concerned with a lower form of art, we need not worry—but, in passing, is it not extraordinary that plays on the stage are often better than they are in the study, and that the introduction of a bunch of rather ambitious and nervous men and women should add anything to our understanding of Shakespeare and Chekov?

No, the novelist has difficulties enough, and today we shall examine two of his devices for solving them—instinctive devices, for his methods when working are seldom the same as the methods we use when examining his work. The first device is the use of different kinds of characters. The second is connected with the point of view.

I. We may divide characters into flat and round.

Flat characters were called "humorous" in the seventeenth century, and are sometimes called types, and sometimes caricatures. In their purest form, they are constructed round a single idea or quality: when there is more than one factor in them, we get the beginning of the curve towards the round. The really flat character can be expressed in one sentence such as "I never will desert Mr. Micawber." There is Mrs. Micawber—she says she won't desert Mr. Micawber, she doesn't, and there she is. Or: "I must conceal, even by subterfuges, the poverty of my master's house." There is Caleb Balderstone in *The Bride of Lammermoor*. He does not use the actual phrase, but it completely describes him; he has no existence outside it, no pleasures, none of the private lusts and aches that must complicate the most consistent of servitors. Whatever he does, wherever he goes, whatever lies he tells or plates he breaks, it is to conceal the poverty of his master's house. It is not his *idée fixe,* because there is nothing in him into which the idea can be fixed. He is the idea, and such life as he possesses radiates from its edges and from the scintillations it strikes when other elements in the novel impinge. Or take Proust. There are numerous flat characters in Proust, such as the Princess of Parma, or Legrandin. Each can be expressed in a single sentence, the Princess's sentence being, "I must be particularly careful to be kind." She does nothing except to be particularly careful, and those of the other characters who are more complex than herself easily see through the kindness, since it is only a by-product of the carefulness.

One great advantage of flat characters is that they are easily recognized whenever they come in—recognized by the reader's emotional eye, not by the visual eye, which merely notes the recurrence of a proper name. In Russian novels, where they so seldom occur, they would be a decided help. It is a convenience for an author when he can strike with his full force at once, and flat characters are very useful to him, since they never need reintroducing, never run away, have not to be watched for development, and provide their own atmosphere—little luminous disks of a pre-arranged size, pushed hither and thither like counters across the void or between the stars; most satisfactory.

A second advantage is that they are easily remembered by the reader afterwards. They remain in his mind as unalterable for the reason that they were not changed by circumstances; they moved through circumstances, which gives them in retrospect a comforting quality, and preserves them when the book that produced them may decay. The Countess in *Evan Harrington* furnishes a good little example here. Let us compare our memories of her with our memories of Becky Sharp. We do not remember what the Countess did or what she passed through. What is clear is her figure and the formula that surrounds it, namely, "Proud as we are of dear papa, we must conceal his memory." All her rich humour proceeds from this. She is a flat character. Becky is round. She, too, is on the make, but she cannot be summed up in a single phrase, and we remember her in connection with the great scenes through which she passed and as modified by those scenes—that is to say, we do not remember her so easily because she waxes and wanes and has facets like a human being. All of us, even the sophisticated, yearn for permanence, and to the unsophisticated permanence is the chief excuse for a work of art. We all want books to endure, to be refuges, and their inhabitants to be always the same, and flat characters tend to justify themselves on this account.

All the same, critics who have their eyes fixed severely upon daily life—as were our eyes last week—have very little patience with such renderings of human nature. Queen Victoria, they argue, cannot be summed up in a single sentence, so what excuse remains for Mrs. Micawber? One of our foremost writers, Mr. Norman Douglas, is a critic of this type, and the passage from him which I will quote puts the case against flat characters in a forcible fashion. The passage occurs in an open letter to D. H. Lawrence, with whom he is quarrelling: a doughty pair of combatants, the hardness of whose hitting makes the rest of us feel like a lot of ladies up in a pavilion. He complains that Lawrence, in a biography, has falsified the picture by employing "the novelist's touch," and he goes on to define what this is:

> It consists, I should say, in a failure to realize the complexities of the ordinary human mind; it selects for literary purposes two or three facets of a man or woman, generally the most spectacular, and therefore useful ingredients of their character and disregards all the others. Whatever fails to fit in with these specially chosen traits is eliminated—must be eliminated, for otherwise the description would not hold water. Such and such are the data: everything incompatible with those data has to go by the board. It follows that the novelist's touch argues, often logically, from a wrong premise: it takes what it

likes and leaves the rest. The facets may be correct as far as they go but there are too few of them: what the author says may be true and yet by no means the truth That is the novelist's touch. It falsifies life.

Well, the novelist's touch as thus defined is, of course, bad in biography, for no human being is simple. But in a novel it has its place: a novel that is at all complex often requires flat people as well as round, and the outcome of their collisions parallels life more accurately than Mr. Douglas implies. The case of Dickens is significant. Dickens' people are nearly all flat (Pip and David Copperfield attempt roundness, but so diffidently that they seem more like bubbles than solids). Nearly every one can be summed up in a sentence, and yet there is this wonderful feeling of human depth. Probably the immense vitality of Dickens causes his characters to vibrate a little, so that they borrow his life and appear to lead one of their own. It is a conjuring trick; at any moment we may look at Mr. Pickwick edgeways and find him no thicker than a gramophone record. But we never get the sideway view. Mr. Pickwick is far too adroit and well-trained. He always has the air of weighing something, and when he is put into the cupboard of the young ladies' school he seems as heavy as Falstaff in the buck-basket at Windsor. Part of the genius of Dickens is that he does use types and caricatures, people whom we recognize the instant they re-enter, and yet achieves effects that are not mechanical and a vision of humanity that is not shallow. Those who dislike Dickens have an excellent case. He ought to be bad. He is actually one of our big writers, and his immense success with types suggests that there may be more in flatness than the severer critics admit.

Or take H. G. Wells. With the possible exceptions of Kipps and the aunt in *Tono Bungay,* all Wells' characters are as flat as a photograph. But the photographs are agitated with such vigour that we forget their complexities lie on the surface and would disappear if it were scratched or curled up. A Wells character cannot indeed be summed up in a single phrase; he is tethered much more to observation, he does not create types. Nevertheless his people seldom pulsate by their own strength. It is the deft and powerful hands of their maker that shake them and trick the reader into a sense of depth. Good but imperfect novelists, like Wells and Dickens, are very clever at transmitting force. The part of their novel that is alive galvanizes the part that is not, and causes the characters to jump about and speak in a convincing way. They are quite different from the perfect novelist who touches all his material directly, who seems to pass the creative finger down every sentence and into every word. Richardson, Defoe, Jane Austen, are perfect in this particular way; their work may not be great but their hands are always upon it; there is not the tiny interval between the touching of the button and the sound of the bell which occurs in novels where the characters are not under direct control.

For we must admit that flat people are not in

themselves as big achievements as round ones, and also that they are best when they are comic. A serious or tragic flat character is apt to be a bore. Each time he enters crying "Revenge!" or "My heart bleeds for humanity!" or whatever his formula is, our hearts sink. One of the romances of a popular contemporary writer is constructed round a Sussex farmer who says, "I'll plough up that bit of gorse." There is the farmer, there is the gorse; he says he'll plough it up, he does plough it up, but it is not like saying "I'll never desert Mr. Micawber," because we are so bored by his consistency that we do not care whether he succeeds with the gorse or fails. If his formula were analysed and connected up with the rest of the human outfit, we should not be bored any longer, the formula would cease to be the man and become an obsession in the man; that is to say he would have turned from a flat farmer into a round one. It is only round people who are fit to perform tragically for any length of time and can move us to any feelings except humour and appropriateness.

So now let us desert these two-dimensional people, and by way of transition to the round, let us go to *Mansfield Park,* and look at Lady Bertram, sitting on her sofa with pug. Pug is flat, like most animals in fiction. He is once represented as straying into a rose-bed in a cardboard kind of way, but that is all, and during most of the book his mistress seems to be cut out of the same simple material as her dog. Lady Bertram's formula is, "I am kindly, but must not be fatigued," and she functions out of it. But at the end there is a catastrophe. Her two daughters come to grief—to the worst grief known to Miss Austen's universe, far worse than the Napoleonic wars. Julia elopes; Maria, who is unhappily married, runs off with a lover. What is Lady Bertram's reaction? The sentence describing it is significant: "Lady Bertram did not think deeply, but, guided by Sir Thomas, she thought justly on all important points, and she saw therefore in all its enormity, what had happened, and neither endeavoured herself, nor required Fanny to advise her, to think little of guilt and infamy." These are strong words, and they used to worry me because I thought Jane Austen's moral sense was getting out of hand. She may, and of course does, deprecate guilt and infamy herself, and she duly causes all possible distress in the minds of Edmund and Fanny, but has she any right to agitate calm, consistent Lady Bertram? Is not it like giving pug three faces and setting him to guard the gates of Hell? Ought not her ladyship to remain on the sofa saying, "This is a dreadful and sadly exhausting business about Julia and Maria, but where is Fanny gone? I have dropped another stitch"?

I used to think this, through misunderstanding Jane Austen's method—exactly as Scott misunderstood it when he congratulated her for painting on a square of ivory. She is a miniaturist, but never two-dimensional. All her characters are round, or capable of rotundity. Even Miss Bates has a mind, even Elizabeth Eliot a heart, and Lady Bertram's moral fervour ceases to vex us when we realize this: the disk has suddenly extended and become a little globe. When the novel is closed, Lady Bertram goes back to the flat, it is true; the dominant impression she leaves can be summed up in a formula. But that is not how Jane Austen conceived her, and the freshness of her reappearances are due to this. Why do the characters in Jane Austen give us a slightly new pleasure each time they come in, as opposed to the merely repetitive pleasure that is caused by a character in Dickens? Why do they combine so well in a conversation, and draw one another out without seeming to do so, and never perform? The answer to this question can be put in several ways: that, unlike Dickens, she was a real artist, that she never stooped to caricature, etc. But the best reply is that her characters though smaller than his are more highly organized. They function all round, and even if her plot made greater demands on them than it does, they would still be adequate. Suppose that Louisa Musgrove had broken her neck on the Cobb. The description of her death would have been feeble and ladylike—physical violence is quite beyond Miss Austen's powers—but the survivors would have reacted properly as soon as the corpse was carried away, they would have brought into view new sides of their character, and though *Persuasion* would have been spoiled as a book, we should know more than we do about Captain Wentworth and Anne. All the Jane Austen characters are ready for an extended life, for a life which the scheme of her books seldom requires them to lead, and that is why they lead their actual lives so satisfactorily. Let us return to Lady Bertram and the crucial sentence. See how subtly it modulates from her formula into an area where the formula does not work. "Lady Bertram did not think deeply." Exactly: as per formula. "But guided by Sir Thomas she thought justly on all important points." Sir Thomas' guidance, which is part of the formula, remains, but it pushes her ladyship towards an independent and undesired morality. "She saw therefore in all its enormity what had happened." This is the moral fortissimo—very strong but carefully introduced. And then follows a most artful decrescendo, by means of negatives. "She neither endeavoured herself, nor required Fanny to advise her, to think little of guilt or infamy." The formula is reappearing, because as a rule she does try to minimize trouble, and does require Fanny to advise her how to do this; indeed Fanny has done nothing else for the last ten years. The words, though they are negatived, remind us of this, her normal state is again in view, and she has in a single sentence been inflated into a round character and collapsed back into a flat one. How Jane Austen can write! In a few words she has extended Lady Bertram, and by so doing she has increased the probability of the elopements of Maria and Julia. I say probability because the elopements belong to the domain of violent physical action, and here, as already indicated, Jane Austen is feeble and ladylike. Except in her schoolgirl novels, she cannot stage a crash. Everything violent has to take place "off"—Louisa's accident and

Marianne Dashwood's putrid throat are the nearest exceptions—and consequently all the comments on the elopement must be sincere and convincing, otherwise we should doubt whether it occurred. Lady Bertram helps us to believe that her daughters have run away, and they have to run away, or there would be no apotheosis for Fanny. It is a little point, and a little sentence, yet it shows us how delicately a great novelist can modulate into the round.

All through her works we find these characters, apparently so simple and flat, never needing reintroduction and yet never out of their depth—Henry Tilney, Mr. Woodhouse, Charlotte Lucas. She may label her characters "Sense," "Pride," "Sensibility," "Prejudice," but they are not tethered to those qualities.

As for the round characters proper, they have already been defined by implication and no more need be said. All I need do is to give some examples of people in books who seem to me round so that the definition can be tested afterwards:

All the principal characters in *War and Peace,* all the Dostoevsky characters, and some of the Proust—for example, the old family servant, the Duchess of Guermantes, M. de Charlus, and Saint Loup; Madame Bovary—who, like Moll Flanders, has her book to herself, and can expand and secrete unchecked; some people in Thackeray—for instance, Becky and Beatrix; some in Fielding—Parson Adams, Tom Jones; and some in Charlotte Brontë, most particularly Lucy Snowe. (And many more—this is not a catalogue.) The test of a round character is whether it is capable of surprising in a convincing way. If it never surprises, it is flat. If it does not convince, it is a flat pretending to be round. It has the incalculability of life about it—life within the pages of a book. And by using it sometimes alone, more often in combination with the other kind, the novelist achieves his task of acclimatization and harmonizes the human race with the other aspects of his work.

II. Now for the second device: the point of view from which the story may be told.

To some critics this is the fundamental device of novel-writing. "The whole intricate question of method, in the craft of fiction," says Mr. Percy Lubbock, "I take to be governed by the question of the *point of view*—the question of the relation in which the narrator stands to the story." And his book *The Craft of Fiction* examines various points of view with genius and insight. The novelist, he says, can either describe the characters from outside, as an impartial or partial onlooker; or he can assume omniscience and describe them from within; or he can place himself in the position of one of them and affect to be in the dark as to the motives of the rest; or there are certain intermediate attitudes.

Those who follow him will lay a sure foundation for the aesthetics of fiction—a foundation which I cannot for a moment promise. This is a ramshackly survey and for me the "whole intricate question of method" resolves itself not into formulae but into the power of the writer to bounce the reader into accepting what he says—a power which Mr. Lubbock admits and admires, but locates at the edge of the problem instead of at the centre. I should put it plumb in the centre. Look how Dickens bounces us in *Bleak House.* Chapter I of *Bleak House* is omniscient. Dickens takes us into the Court of Chancery and rapidly explains all the people there. In Chapter II he is partially omniscient. We still use his eyes, but for some unexplained reason they begin to grow weak: he can explain Sir Leicester Dedlock to us, part of Lady Dedlock but not all, and nothing of Mr. Tulkinghorn. In Chapter III he is even more reprehensible: he goes straight across into the dramatic method and inhabits a young lady, Esther Summerson. "I have a great deal of difficulty in beginning to write my portion of these pages, for I know I am not clever," pipes up Esther, and continues in this strain with consistency and competence, so long as she is allowed to hold the pen. At any moment the author of her being may snatch it from her, and run about taking notes himself, leaving her seated goodness knows where, and employed we do not care how. Logically, *Bleak House* is all to pieces, but Dickens bounces us, so that we do not mind the shiftings of the view-point.

Critics are more apt to object than readers. Zealous for the novel's eminence, they are a little too apt to look out for problems that shall be peculiar to it, and differentiate it from the drama; they feel it ought to have its own technical troubles before it can be accepted as an independent art: and since the problem of a point of view certainly is peculiar to the novel they have rather overstressed it. I do not myself think it is so important as a proper mixture of characters—a problem which the dramatist is up against also. And the novelist must bounce us; that is imperative.

Let us glance at two other examples of a shifting view-point.

The eminent French writer, André Gide, has published a novel called *Les Faux Monnayeurs*[1]—for all its modernity, this novel of Gide's has one aspect in common with *Bleak House:* it is all to pieces logically. Sometimes the author is omniscient: he explains everything, he stands back, *"il juge ses personnages";* at other times his omniscience is partial; yet again he is dramatic, and causes the story to be told through the diary of one of the characters. There is the same absence of view-point, but whereas in Dickens it was instinctive, in Gide it is sophisticated; he expatiates too much about the jolts. The novelist who betrays too much interest in his own method can never be more than interesting; he has given up the creation of character and summoned us to help analyse his own mind, and a heavy drop in the emotional thermometer results. *Les Faux Monnayeurs* is among the more interesting of recent works: not among the vital: and greatly as we shall have to admire it as a fabric we cannot praise it unrestrictedly now.

For our second example we must again glance at

[1] Translated by Dorothy Bussy as *The Counterfeiters,* Knopf.

War and Peace. Here the result is vital: we are bounced up and down Russia—omniscient, semi-omniscient, dramatized here or there as the moment dictates—and at the end we have accepted it all. Mr. Lubbock does not, it is true: great as he finds the book, he would find it greater if it had a view-point; he feels Tolstoy has not pulled his full weight. I feel that the rules of the game of writing are not like this. A novelist can shift his view-point if it comes off, and it came off with Dickens and Tolstoy. Indeed this power to expand and contract perception (of which the shifting view-point is a symptom), this right to intermittent knowledge:—I find it one of the great advantages of the novel-form, and it has a parallel in our perception of life. We are stupider at some times than others; we can enter into people's minds occasionally but not always, because our own minds get tired; and this intermittence lends in the long run variety and colour to the experiences we receive. A quantity of novelists, English novelists especially, have behaved like this to the people in their books: played fast and loose with them, and I cannot see why they should be censured.

They must be censured if we catch them at it at the time. That is quite true, and out of it arises another question: may the writer take the reader into his confidence about his characters? Answer has already been indicated: better not. It is dangerous, it generally leads to a drop in the temperature, to intellectual and emotional laxity, and worse still to facetiousness, and to a friendly invitation to see how the figures hook up behind. "Doesn't A look nice—she always was my favourite." "Let's think of why B does that—perhaps there's more in him than meets the eye—yes, see—he has a heart of gold—having given you this peep at it I'll pop it back—I don't think he's noticed." "And C—he always was the mystery man." Intimacy is gained but at the expense of illusion and nobility. It is like standing a man a drink so that he may not criticize your opinions. With all respect to Fielding and Thackeray it is devastating, it is bar-parlour chattiness, and nothing has been more harmful to the novels of the past. To take your reader into your confidence about the universe is a different thing. It is not dangerous for a novelist to draw back from his characters, as Hardy and Conrad do, and to generalize about the conditions under which he thinks life is carried on. It is confidences about the individual people that do harm, and beckon the reader away from the people to an examination of the novelist's mind. Not much is ever found in it at such a moment, for it is never in the creative state: the mere process of saying, "Come along, let's have a chat," has cooled it down.

Our comments on human beings must now come to an end. They may take fuller shape when we come to discuss the plot.

Five

THE PLOT

"CHARACTER," says Aristotle, "gives us qualities, but it is in actions—what we do—that we are happy or the reverse." We have already decided that Aristotle is wrong and now we must face the consequences of disagreeing with him. "All human happiness and misery," says Aristotle, "take the form of action." We know better. We believe that happiness and misery exist in the secret life, which each of us leads privately and to which (in his characters) the novelist has access. And by the secret life we mean the life for which there is no external evidence, not, as is vulgarly supposed, that which is revealed by a chance word or a sigh. A chance word or sigh are just as much evidence as a speech or a murder: the life they reveal ceases to be secret and enters the realm of action.

There is, however, no occasion to be hard on Aristotle. He had read few novels and no modern ones—the *Odyssey* but not *Ulysses*—he was by temperament apathetic to secrecy, and indeed regarded the human mind as a sort of tub from which everything can finally be extracted; and when he wrote the words quoted above he had in view the drama, where no doubt they hold true. In the drama all human happiness and misery does and must take the form of action. Otherwise its existence remains unknown, and this is the great difference between the drama and the novel.

The speciality of the novel is that the writer can talk about his characters as well as through them or can arrange for us to listen when they talk to themselves. He has access to self-communings, and from that level he can descend even deeper and peer into the subconscious. A man does not talk to himself quite truly—not even to himself; the happiness or misery that he secretly feels proceeds from causes that he cannot quite explain, because as soon as he raises them to the level of the explicable they lose their native quality. The novelist has a real pull here. He can show the subconscious short-circuiting straight into action (the dramatist can do this too); he can also show it in its relation to soliloquy. He commands all the secret life, and he must not be robbed of this privilege. "How did the writer know that?" it is sometimes said. "What's his standpoint? He is not being consistent, he's shifting his point of view from the limited to the omniscient, and now he's edging back again." Questions like these have too much the atmosphere of the law courts about them. All that matters to the reader is whether the shifting of attitude and the secret life are convincing, whether it is *πιθανόν* in fact, and with his favourite word ringing in his ears Aristotle may retire.

However, he leaves us in some confusion, for what, with this enlargement of human nature, is going to become of the plot? In most literary works there are two elements: human individuals, whom we have recently discussed, and the element vaguely called art. Art we have also dallied with, but with a very low form of it: the story: the chopped-off length of the tapeworm of time. Now we arrive at a much higher aspect: the plot, and the plot, instead of finding human beings more or less cut to its requirements, as they are in the drama, finds them enormous, shadowy and intractable, and three-quarters hidden like an iceberg. In vain it points out to these unwieldy creatures the advantages of the triple process of complication, crisis, and solution so persuasively expounded by Aristotle. A few of them rise and comply, and a novel which ought to have been a play is the result. But there is no general response. They want to sit apart and brood or something, and the plot (whom I here visualize as a sort of higher government official) is concerned at their lack of public spirit: "This will not do," it seems to say. "Individualism is a most valuable quality; indeed my own position depends upon individuals; I have always admitted as much freely. Nevertheless there are certain limits, and those limits are being overstepped. Characters must not brood too long, they must not waste time running up and down ladders in their own insides, they must contribute, or higher interests will be jeopardised." How well one knows that phrase, "a contribution to the plot"!

It is accorded, and of necessity, by the people in a drama: how necessary is it in a novel?

Let us define a plot. We have defined a story as a narrative of events arranged in their time-sequence. A plot is also a narrative of events, the emphasis falling on causality. "The king died and then the queen died" is a story. "The king died, and then the queen died of grief" is a plot. The time-sequence is preserved, but the sense of causality overshadows it. Or again: "The queen died, no one knew why, until it was discovered that it was through grief at the death of the king." This is a plot with a mystery in it, a form capable of high development. It suspends the time-sequence, it moves as far away from the story as its limitations will allow. Consider the death of the queen. If it is in a story we say "and then?" If it is in a plot we ask "why?" That is the fundamental difference between these two aspects of the novel. A plot cannot be told to a gaping audience of cave-men or to a tyrannical sultan or to their modern descendant the movie-public. They can only be kept awake by "and then—and then——" They can only supply curiosity. But a plot demands intelligence and memory also.

Curiosity is one of the lowest of the human faculties. You will have noticed in daily life that when people are inquisitive they nearly always have bad memories and are usually stupid at bottom. The man who begins by asking you how many brothers and sisters you have is never a sympathetic character, and if you meet him in a year's time he will probably ask you how many brothers and sisters you have, his mouth again sagging open, his eyes still bulging from his head. It is difficult to be friends with such a man, and for two inquisitive people to be friends must be impossible. Curiosity by itself takes us a very little way, nor does it take us far into the novel—only as far as the story. If we would grasp the plot we must add intelligence and memory.

Intelligence first. The intelligent novel-reader, unlike the inquisitive one who just runs his eye over a new fact, mentally picks it up. He sees it from two points of view: isolated, and related to the other facts that he has read on previous pages. Probably he does not understand it, but he does not expect to do so yet awhile. The facts in a highly organized novel (like *The Egoist*) are often of the nature of cross-correspondences and the ideal spectator cannot expect to view them properly until he is sitting up on a hill at the end. This element of surprise or mystery—the detective element as it is sometimes rather emptily called—is of great importance in a plot. It occurs through a suspension of the time-sequence; a mystery is a pocket in time, and it occurs crudely, as in "Why did the queen die?" and more subtly in half-explained gestures and words, the true meaning of which only dawns pages ahead. Mystery is essential to a plot, and cannot be appreciated without intelligence. To the curious it is just another "and then——" To appreciate a mystery, part of the mind must be left behind, brooding, while the other part goes marching on.

That brings us to our second qualification: memory.

Memory and intelligence are closely connected, for unless we remember we cannot understand. If by the time the queen dies we have forgotten the existence of the king we shall never make out what killed her. The plot-maker expects us to remember, we expect him to leave no loose ends. Every action or word ought to count; it ought to be economical and spare; even when complicated it should be organic and free from dead-matter. It may be difficult or easy, it may and should contain mysteries, but it ought not to mislead. And over it, as it unfolds, will hover the memory of the reader (that dull glow of the mind of which intelligence is the bright advancing edge) and will constantly rearrange and reconsider, seeing new clues, new chains of cause and effect, and the final sense (if the plot has been a fine one) will not be of clues or chains, but of something aesthetically compact, something which might have been shown by the novelist straight away, only if he had shown it straight away it would never have become beautiful. We come up against beauty here—for the first time in our inquiry: beauty at which a novelist should never aim, though he fails if he does not achieve it. I will conduct beauty to her proper place later on. Meanwhile please accept her as part of a completed plot. She looks a little surprised at being there, but beauty ought to look a little surprised: it is the emotion that best suits her face, as Botticelli knew when he painted her risen from the waves, between the winds and the flowers. The beauty who does not look surprised, who accepts her position as her due—she reminds us too much of a prima donna.

But let us get back to the plot, and we will do so via George Meredith.

Meredith is not the great name he was twenty or thirty years ago, when much of the universe and all Cambridge trembled. I remember how depressed I used to be by a line in one of his poems: "We live but to be sword or block." I did not want to be either and I knew that I was not a sword. It seems though that there was no real cause for depression, for Meredith is himself now rather in the trough of a wave, and though fashion will turn and raise him a bit, he will never be the spiritual power he was about the year 1900. His philosophy has not worn well. His heavy attacks on sentimentality—they bore the present generation, which pursues the same quarry but with neater instruments, and is apt to suspect anyone carrying a blunderbuss of being a sentimentalist himself. And his visions of Nature—they do not endure like Hardy's, there is too much Surrey about them, they are fluffy and lush. He could no more write the opening chapter of *The Return of the Native* than Box Hill could visit Salisbury Plain. What is really tragic and enduring in the scenery of England was hidden from him, and so is what is really tragic in life. When he gets serious and noble-minded there is a strident overtone, a bullying that becomes distressing. I feel indeed that he was like Tennyson in one respect: through not taking himself quietly enough he strained his inside. And his novels: most of the social values are faked. The tailors are not tailors, the cricket matches are not cricket, the railway trains do not even seem to be trains, the county families give the air of having been only just that moment unpacked, scarcely in position before the action starts, the straw still clinging to their beards. It is surely very odd, the social scene in which his characters are set: it is partly due to his fantasy, which is legitimate, but partly a chilly fake, and wrong. What with the faking, what with the preaching, which was never agreeable and is now said to be hollow, and what with the home counties posing as the universe, it is no wonder Meredith now lies in the trough. And yet he is in one way a great novelist. He is the finest contriver that English fiction has ever produced, and any lecture on plot must do homage to him.

Meredith's plots are not closely knit. We cannot describe the action of *Harry Richmond* in a phrase, as we can that of *Great Expectations,* though both books turn on the mistake made by a young man as to the sources of his fortune. A Meredithian plot is not a temple to the tragic or even to the comic Muse, but rather resembles a series of kiosks most artfully placed among wooded slopes, which his people reach by their own impetus, and from which they emerge with altered aspect. Incident springs out of character, and having occurred it alters that character. People and events are closely connected, and he does it by means of these contrivances. They are often delightful, sometimes touching, always unexpected. This shock, followed by the feeling, "Oh, that's all right," is a sign that all is well with the plot: characters, to be real, ought to run smoothly, but a plot ought to cause surprise. The horse-whipping of Dr. Shrapnel in *Beauchamp's Career* is a surprise. We know that Everard Romfrey must dislike Shrapnel, must hate and misunderstand his radicalism, and be jealous of his influence over Beauchamp: we watch too the growth of the misunderstanding over Rosamund, we watch the intrigues of Cecil Baskelett. As far as characters go, Meredith plays with his cards on the table, but when the incident comes what a shock it gives us and the characters too! The tragi-comic business of one old man whipping another from the highest motives—it reacts upon all their world, and transforms all the personages of the book. It is not the centre of *Beauchamp's Career,* which indeed has no centre. It is essentially a contrivance, a door through which the book is made to pass, emerging in an altered form. Towards the close, when Beauchamp is drowned and Shrapnel and Romfrey are reconciled over his body, there is an attempt to elevate the plot to Aristotelian symmetry, to turn the novel into a temple wherein dwells interpretation and peace. Meredith fails here: *Beauchamp's Career* remains a series of contrivances (the visit to France is another of them), but contrivances that spring from the characters and react upon them.

And now briefly to illustrate the mystery element

in the plot: the formula of "The queen died, it was afterwards discovered through grief." I will take an example, not from Dickens (though *Great Expectations* provides a fine one), nor from Conan Doyle (whom my priggishness prevents me from enjoying), but again from Meredith: an example of a concealed emotion from the admirable plot of *The Egoist:* it occurs in the character of Laetitia Dale.

We are told, at first, all that passes in Laetitia's mind. Sir Willoughby has twice jilted her, she is sad, resigned. Then, for dramatic reasons, her mind is hidden from us, it develops naturally enough, but does not re-emerge until the great midnight scene where he asks her to marry him because he is not sure about Clara, and this time, a changed woman, Laetitia says "No." Meredith has concealed the change. It would have spoiled his high comedy if we had been kept in touch with it throughout. Sir Willoughby has to have a series of crashes, to catch at this and that, and find everything rickety. We should not enjoy the fun, in fact it would be boorish, if we saw the author preparing the booby traps beforehand, so Laetitia's apathy has been hidden from us. This is one of the countless examples in which either plot or character has to suffer, and Meredith with his unerring good sense here lets the plot triumph.

As an example of mistaken triumph, I think of a slip—it is no more than a slip—which Charlotte Brontë makes in *Villette.* She allows Lucy Snowe to conceal from the reader her discovery that Dr. John is the same as her old playmate Graham. When it comes out, we do get a good plot thrill, but too much at the expense of Lucy's character. She has seemed, up to then, the spirit of integrity, and has, as it were, laid herself under a moral obligation to narrate all that she knows. That she stoops to suppress is a little distressing, though the incident is too trivial to do her any permanent harm.

Sometimes a plot triumphs too completely. The characters have to suspend their natures at every turn, or else are so swept away by the course of Fate that our sense of their reality is weakened. We shall find instances of this in a writer who is far greater than Meredith, and yet less successful as a novelist—Thomas Hardy. Hardy seems to me essentially a poet, who conceives of his novels from an enormous height. They are to be tragedies or tragi-comedies, they are to give out the sound of hammer-strokes as they proceed; in other words Hardy arranges events with emphasis on causality, the ground plan is a plot, and the characters are ordered to acquiesce in its requirements. Except in the person of Tess (who conveys the feeling that she is greater than destiny) this aspect of his work is unsatisfactory. His characters are involved in various snares, they are finally bound hand and foot, there is ceaseless emphasis on fate, and yet, for all the sacrifices made to it, we never see the action as a living thing as we see it in *Antigone* or *Berenice* or *The Cherry Orchard*. The fate above us, not the fate working through us—that is what is eminent and memorable in the Wessex novels.

Egdon Heath before Eustacia Vye has set foot upon it. The woods without the Woodlanders. The downs above Budmouth Regis with the royal princesses, still asleep, driving across them through the dawn. Hardy's success in *The Dynasts* (where he uses another medium) is complete, there the hammer-strokes are heard, cause and effect enchain the characters despite their struggles, complete contact between the actors and the plot is established. But in the novels, though the same superb and terrible machine works, it never catches humanity in its teeth; there is some vital problem that has not been answered, or even posed, in the misfortunes of Jude the Obscure. In other words the characters have been required to contribute too much to the plot; except in their rustic humours, their vitality has been impoverished, they have gone dry and thin. This, as far as I can make out, is the flaw running through Hardy's novels: he has emphasized causality more strongly than his medium permits. As a poet and prophet and visualizer George Meredith is nothing by his side—just a suburban roarer—but Meredith did know what the novel could stand, where the plot could dun the characters for a contribution, where it must let them function as they liked. And the moral—well, I see no moral, because the work of Hardy is my home and that of Meredith cannot be: still the moral from the point of these lectures is again unfavourable to Aristotle. In the novel, all human happiness and misery does not take the form of action, it seeks means of expression other than through the plot, it must not be rigidly canalized.

In the losing battle that the plot fights with the characters, it often takes a cowardly revenge. Nearly all novels are feeble at the end. This is because the plot requires to be wound up. Why is this necessary? Why is there not a convention which allows a novelist to stop as soon as he feels muddled or bored? Alas, he has to round things off, and usually the characters go dead while he is at work, and our final impression of them is through deadness. *The Vicar of Wakefield* is in this way a typical novel, so clever and fresh in the first half, up to the painting of the family group with Mrs. Primrose as Venus, and then so wooden and imbecile. Incidents and people that occurred at first for their own sake now have to contribute to the *dénouement*. In the end even the author feels he is being a little foolish. "Nor can I go on," he says, "without a reflection on those accidental meetings which, though they happen every day, seldom excite our surprise but upon some extraordinary occasion." Goldsmith is of course a lightweight, but most novels do fail here—there is this disastrous standstill while logic takes over the command from flesh and blood. If it was not for death and marriage I do not know how the average novelist would conclude. Death and marriage are almost his only connection between his characters and his plot, and the reader is more ready to meet him here, and take a bookish view of them, provided they occur later on in the book: the writer, poor fellow, must be allowed to finish up somehow, he has his living to get like anyone else, so no wonder that nothing is heard but hammering and screwing.

This—as far as one can generalize—is the inherent defect of novels: they go off at the end: and there are two explanations of it: firstly, failure of pep, which threatens the novelist like all workers: and secondly, the difficulty which we have been discussing. The characters have been getting out of hand, laying foundations and declining to build on them afterwards, and now the novelist has to labour personally, in order that the job may be done to time. He pretends that the characters are acting for him. He keeps mentioning their names and using inverted commas. But the characters are gone or dead.

The plot, then, is the novel in its logical intellectual aspect: it requires mystery, but the mysteries are solved later on: the reader may be moving about in worlds unrealized, but the novelist has no misgivings. He is competent, poised above his work, throwing a beam of light here, popping on a cap of invisibility there, and (*qua* plot-maker) continually negotiating with himself *qua* character-monger as to the best effect to be produced. He plans his book beforehand: or anyhow he stands above it, his interest in cause and effect give him an air of predetermination.

And now we must ask ourselves whether the framework thus produced is the best possible for a novel. After all, why has a novel to be planned? Cannot it grow? Why need it close, as a play closes? Cannot it open out? Instead of standing above his work and controlling it, cannot the novelist throw himself into it and be carried along to some goal that he does not foresee? The plot is exciting and may be beautiful, yet is it not a fetish, borrowed from the drama, from the spatial limitations of the stage? Cannot fiction devise a framework that is not so logical yet more suitable to its genius?

Modern writers say that it can, and we will now examine a recent example—a violent onslaught on the plot as we have defined it: a constructive attempt to put something in the place of the plot.

I have already mentioned the novel in question: *Les Faux Monnayeurs* by André Gide. It contains within its covers both the methods. Gide has also published the diary he kept while he was writing the novel, and there is no reason why he should not publish in the future the impressions he had when rereading both the diary and the novel, and in the future-perfect a still more final synthesis in which the diary, the novel, and his impressions of both will interact. He is indeed a little more solemn than an author should be about the whole caboodle, but regarded as a caboodle it is excessively interesting, and repays careful study by critics.

We have, in the first place, a plot in *Les Faux Monnayeurs* of the logical objective type that we have been considering—a plot, or rather fragments of plots. The main fragment concerns a young man called Olivier—a charming, touching and lovable character, who misses happiness, and then recovers it after an excellently contrived *dénouement;* confers it also; this fragment has a wonderful radiance and "lives," if I may use so coarse a word, it is a successful creation on familiar lines. But it is by no means the centre of the book. No more are the other logical fragments—that which concerns Georges, Olivier's schoolboy brother, who passes false coin, and is instrumental in driving a fellow-pupil to suicide. (Gide gives us his sources for all this in his diary, he got the idea of Georges from a boy whom he caught trying to steal a book off a stall, the gang of coiners were caught at Rouen, and the suicide of children took place at Clermont-Ferrand, etc.) Neither Olivier, nor Georges, nor Vincent, a third brother, nor Bernard their friend is the centre of the book. We come nearer to it in Edouard. Edouard is a novelist. He bears the same relation to Gide as Clissold does to Wells. I dare not be more precise. Like Gide, he keeps a diary, like Gide he is writing a book called *Les Faux Monnayeurs,* and like Clissold he is disavowed. Edouard's diary is printed in full. It begins before the plot-fragments, continues during them, and forms the bulk of Gide's book. Edouard is not just a chronicler. He is an actor too; indeed it is he who rescues Olivier and is rescued by him; we leave those two in happiness.

But that is still not the centre. The nearest to the centre lies in a discussion about the art of the novel. Edouard is holding forth to Bernard his secretary and some friends. He has said (what we all accept as commonplace) that truth in life and truth in a novel are not identical, and then he goes on to say that he wants to write a book which shall include both sorts of truth.

"And what is its subject?" asked Sophroniska.

"There is none," said Edouard sharply. "My novel has no subject. No doubt that sounds foolish. Let us say, if you prefer, that it will not have 'a' subject. . . . 'A slice of life,' the naturalistic school used to say. The mistake that school made was always to cut its slice in the same direction, always lengthwise, in the direction of time. Why not cut it up and down? Or across? As for me, I don't want to cut it at all. You see what I mean. I want to put everything into my novel and not snip off my material either here or there. I have been working for a year, and there is nothing I haven't put in: all I see, all I know, all I can learn from other people's lives and my own."

"My poor man, you will bore your readers to death," cried Laura, unable to restrain her mirth.

"Not at all. To get my effect, I am inventing, as my central character, a novelist, and the subject of my book will be the struggle between what reality offers him and what he tries to make of the offer."

"Have you planned out this book?" asked Sophroniska, trying to keep grave.

"Of course not."

"Why 'of course'?"

"For a book of this type any plan would be unsuitable. The whole of it would go wrong if I decided any detail ahead. I am waiting for reality to dictate to me."

"But I thought you wanted to get away from reality."

"My novelist wants to get away, but I keep pulling him back. To tell the truth, this is my subject: the struggle between facts as proposed by reality, and the ideal reality."

"Do tell us the name of this book," said Laura, in despair.

"Very well. Tell it them, Bernard."

"Les Faux Monnayeurs," said Bernard. "And now will you please tell us who these faux monnayeurs are."

"I haven't the least idea."

Bernard and Laura looked at each other and then at Sophroniska. There was the sound of a deep sigh.

The fact was that ideas about money, depreciation, inflation, forgery, etc., had gradually invaded Edouard's book—just as theories of clothing invade *Sartor Resartus* and even assume the functions of characters. "Has any of you ever had hold of a false coin?" he asked after a pause. "Imagine a ten-franc piece, gold, false. It is actually worth a couple of sous, but it will remain worth ten francs until it is found out. Suppose I begin with the idea that——"

"But why begin with an idea?" burst out Bernard, who was by now in a state of exasperation. "Why not begin with a fact? If you introduce the fact properly, the idea will follow of itself. If I was writing your *Faux Monnayeurs* I should begin with a piece of false money, with the ten-franc piece you were speaking of, and here it is!"

So saying, Bernard pulled a ten-franc piece out of his pocket and flung it on the table.

"There," he remarked. "It rings all right. I got it this morning from the grocer. It's worth more than a couple of sous, as it's coated in gold, but it's actually made of glass. It will become quite transparent in time. No—don't rub it—you're going to spoil my false coin."

Edouard had taken it and was examining it with the utmost attention.

"How did the grocer get it?"

"He doesn't know. He passed it on me for a joke, and then enlightened me, being a decent fellow. He let me have it for five francs. I thought that, since you were writing *Les Faux Monnayeurs,* you ought to see what false money is like, so I got it to show you. Now that you have looked at it, give it me back. I am sorry to see that reality has no interest for you."

"Yes," said Edouard: "it interests me, but it puts me out."

"That's a pity," remarked Bernard.[1]

This passage is the centre of the book. It contains the old thesis of truth in life versus truth in art, and illustrates it very neatly by the arrival of an actual false coin. What is new in it is the attempt to combine the two truths, the proposal that writers should mix themselves up in their material and be rolled over and over by it; they should not try to subdue any longer, they should hope to be subdued, to be carried away. As for a plot—to pot with the plot, break it up, boil it down. Let there be those "formidable erosions of contour" of which Nietzsche speaks. All that is prearranged is false.

Another distinguished critic has agreed with Gide—that old lady in the anecdote who was accused by her nieces of being illogical. For some time she could not be brought to understand what logic was, and when she grasped its true nature she was not so much angry as contemptuous. "Logic! Good gracious! What rubbish!" she exclaimed. "How can I tell what I think till I see what I say?" Her nieces, educated young women, thought that she was *passée;* she was really more up to date than they were.

[1] Paraphrased from *Les Faux Monnayeurs,* pp. 238-246. My version, needless to say, conveys neither the subtlety nor the balance of the original.

Those who are in touch with contemporary France say that the present generation follows the advice of Gide and the old lady and resolutely hurls itself into confusion, and indeed admires English novelists on the ground that they so seldom succeed in what they attempt. Compliments are always delightful, but this particular one is a bit of a back-hander. It is like trying to lay an egg and being told you have produced a paraboloid—more curious than gratifying. And what results when you try to lay a paraboloid, I cannot conceive—perhaps the death of the hen. That seems the danger in Gide's position—he sets out to lay a paraboloid; he is not well advised, if he wants to write subconscious novels, to reason so lucidly and patiently about the subconscious; he is introducing mysticism at the wrong stage of the process. However that is his affair. As a critic he is most stimulating, and the various bundles of words he has called *Les Faux Monnayeurs* will be enjoyed by all who cannot tell what they think till they see what they say, or who weary of the tyranny by the plot and of its alternative, tyranny by characters.

There is clearly something else in view, some other aspect or aspects which we have yet to examine. We may suspect the claim to be consciously subconscious, nevertheless there is a vague and vast residue into which the subconscious enters. Poetry, religion, passion—we have not placed them yet, and since we are critics—only critics—we must try to place them, to catalogue the rainbow. We have already peeped and botanized upon our mothers' graves.

The numbering of the warp and woof of the rainbow must accordingly be attempted and we must now bring our minds to bear on the subject of fantasy.

Six

FANTASY

A COURSE of lectures, if it is to be more than a collection of remarks, must have an idea running through it. It must also have a subject, and the idea ought to run through the subject too. This is so obvious as to sound foolish, but anyone who has tried to lecture will realize that here is a genuine difficulty. A course, like any other collection of words, generates an atmosphere. It has its own apparatus—a lecturer, an audience or provision for one, it occurs at regular intervals, it is announced by printed notices, and it has a financial side, though this last is tactfully concealed. Thus it tends in its parasitic way to lead a life of its own, and it and the idea running through it are apt to move in one direction while the subject steals off in the other.

The idea running through these lectures is by now plain enough: that there are in the novel two forces: human beings and a bundle of various things not human beings, and that it is the novelist's business to adjust these two forces and conciliate their claims. That is plain enough, but does it run through the novel too? Perhaps our subject, namely the books we have read, has stolen away from us while we theorize, like a shadow from an ascending bird. The bird is all right—it climbs, it is consistent and eminent. The shadow is all right—it has flickered across roads and gardens. But the two things resemble one another less and less, they do not touch as they did when the bird rested its toes on the ground. Criticism, especially a critical course, is so misleading. However lofty its intentions and sound its method, its subject slides away from beneath it, imperceptibly away, and lecturer and audience may awake with a start to find that they are carrying on in a distinguished and intelligent manner, but in regions which have nothing to do with anything they have read.

It was this that was worrying Gide, or rather one of the things that was worrying him, for he has an anxious mind. When we try to translate truth out of one sphere into another, whether from life into books or from books into lectures, something happens to truth, it goes wrong, not suddenly when it might be detected, but slowly. That long passage from *Les Faux Monnayeurs* already quoted, may recall the bird to its shadow. It is not possible, after it, to apply the old apparatus any more. There is more in the novel than time or people or logic or any of their derivatives, more even than Fate. And by "more" I do not mean something that excludes these aspects nor something that includes them, embraces them. I mean something that cuts across them like a bar of light, that is intimately connected with them at one place and patiently illumines all their problems, and at another place shoots over or through them as if they did not exist. We shall give that bar of light two names, fantasy and prophecy.

The novels we have now to consider all tell a story, contain characters, and have plots or bits of plots, so we could apply to them the apparatus suited for Fielding or Arnold Bennett. But when I say two of their names—*Tristram Shandy* and *Moby Dick*—it is clear that we must stop and think a moment. The bird and the shadow are too far apart. A new formula must be found: the mere fact that one can mention Tristram and Moby in a single sentence shows it. What an impossible pair! As far apart as the poles. Yes. And like the poles they have one thing in common, which the lands round the equator do not share: an axis. What is essential in Sterne and Melville belongs to this new aspect of fiction: the fantastic-prophetical axis. George Meredith touched it: he was somewhat fantastic. So did Charlotte Brontë: she was a prophetess occasionally. But in neither of these was it essential. Deprive them of it, and a book remains which still resembles *Harry Richmond* or *Shirley*. Deprive Sterne or Melville of it, deprive Peacock or Max Beerbohm or Virginia Woolf or Walter de la Mare or William Beckford or James Joyce or D. H. Lawrence or Swift, and nothing is left at all.

Our easiest approach to a definition of any aspect of fiction is always by considering the sort of demand it makes on the reader. Curiosity for the story, human feelings and a sense of value for the characters, intelligence and memory for the plot. What does fantasy ask of us? It asks us to pay something extra. It compels us to an adjustment that is different to an adjustment required by a work of art, to an additional adjustment. The other novelists say "Here is something that might occur in your lives," the fantasist says "Here's something that could not occur. I must ask you first to accept my book as a whole, and secondly to accept certain things in my book." Many readers can grant the first request, but refuse the second. "One knows a book isn't real," they say, "still one does expect it to be natural, and this angel or midget or ghost or silly delay about the child's birth—no, it is too much." They either retract their original concession and stop reading, or if they do go on it is with complete coldness, and they watch the gambols of the author without realizing how much they may mean to him.

No doubt the above approach is not critically sound. We all know that a work of art is an entity, etc., etc.; it has its own laws which are not those of daily life, anything that suits it is true, so why should any question arise about the angel, etc., except whether it is suitable to its book? Why place an angel on a different basis from a stockbroker? Once in the realm of the fictitious, what difference is there between an apparition and a mortgage? I see the soundness of this argument, but my heart refuses to assent. The general tone of novels is so literal that when the fantastic is introduced it produces a special effect: some readers are thrilled, others choked off: it demands an additional adjustment because of the oddness of its method or subject matter—like a sideshow in an exhibition where you have to pay sixpence as well as the original entrance fee. Some readers pay with delight, it is only for the sideshows that they entered the exhibition, and it is only to them I can now speak. Others refuse with indignation, and these have our sincere regards, for to dislike the fantastic in literature is not to dislike literature. It does not even imply poverty of imagination, only a disinclination to meet certain demands that are made on it. Mr. Asquith (if gossip is correct) could not meet the demands made on him by *Lady into Fox*. He should not have objected, he said, if the fox had become a lady again, but as it was he was left with an uncomfortable dissatisfied feeling. This feeling reflects no discredit either upon an eminent politician or a charming book. It merely means that Mr. Asquith, though a genuine lover of literature, could not pay the additional sixpence—or rather he was willing to pay it but hoped to get it back again at the end.

So fantasy asks us to pay something extra.

Let us now distinguish between fantasy and prophecy.

They are alike in having gods, and unlike in the gods they have. There is in both the sense of mythology which differentiates them from other aspects of our subject. An invocation is again possible. therefore on behalf of fantasy let us now invoke all beings who inhabit the lower air, the shallow water, and the smaller hills, all Fauns and Dryads and slips of the memory, all verbal coincidences, Pans and puns, all that is medieval this side of the grave. When we come to prophecy, we shall utter no invocation, but it will have been to whatever transcends our abilities, even when it is human passion that transcends them, to the deities of India, Greece, Scandinavia and Judaea, to all that is medieval beyond the grave and to Lucifer son of the morning. By their mythologies we shall distinguish these two sorts of novels.

A number of rather small gods then should haunt us today—I would call them fairies if the word were not consecrated to imbecility. (Do you believe in fairies? No, not under any circumstances.) The stuff of daily life will be tugged and strained in various directions, the earth will be given little tilts mischievous or pensive, spotlights will fall on objects that have no reason to anticipate or welcome them, and tragedy herself, though not excluded, will have a fortuitous air as if a word would disarm her. The power of fantasy penetrates into every corner of the universe, but not into the forces that govern it—the stars that are the brain of heaven, the army of unalterable law, remain untouched—and novels of this type have an improvised air, which is the secret of their force and charm. They may contain solid character-drawing, penetrating and bitter criticism of conduct and civilization; yet our simile of the beam of light must remain, and if one god must be invoked specially, let us call upon Hermes—messenger, thief, and conductor of souls to a not-too-terrible hereafter.

You will expect me now to say that a fantastic book asks us to accept the supernatural. I will say it, but reluctantly, because any statement as to their subject matter brings these novels into the claws of critical apparatus, from which it is important that they should be saved. It is truer of them than of most books that we can only know what is in them by reading them, and their appeal is specially personal —they are sideshows inside the main show. So I would rather hedge as much as possible, and say that they ask us to accept either the supernatural or its absence.

A reference to the greatest of them—*Tristram Shandy*—will make this point clear. The supernatural is absent from the Shandy ménage, yet a thousand incidents suggest that it is not far off. It would not be really odd, would it, if the furniture in Mr. Shandy's bedroom, where he retired in despair after hearing the omitted details of his son's birth, should come alive like Belinda's toilette in *The Rape of the Lock,* or that Uncle Toby's drawbridge should lead into Lilliput? There is a charmed stagnation about the whole epic—the more the characters do the less gets done, the less they have to say the more they talk, the harder they think the softer they get, facts have an unholy tendency to unwind and trip up the past instead of begetting the future, as in well-conducted books, and the obstinacy of inanimate objects, like Dr. Slop's bag, is most suspicious. Obviously a god is hidden in *Tristram Shandy,* his name is Muddle, and some readers cannot accept him. Muddle is almost incarnate—quite to reveal his awful features was not Sterne's intention; that is the deity that lurks behind his masterpiece—the army of unutterable muddle, the universe as a hot chestnut. Small wonder that another divine muddler, Dr. Johnson, writing in 1776, should remark, "Nothing odd will do long: *Tristram Shandy* did not last!" Doctor Johnson was not always happy in his literary judgments, but the appropriateness of this one passes belief.

Well, that must serve as our definition of fantasy. It implies the supernatural, but need not express it. Often it does express it, and were that type of classification helpful, we could make a list of the devices which writers of a fantastic turn have used—such as the introduction of a god, ghost, angel, monkey, monster, midget, witch into ordinary life; or the introduction of ordinary men into no man's land, the future, the past, the interior of the earth, the fourth dimension; or divings into and dividings of personality; or finally the device of parody or adaptation. These devices need never grow stale; they will occur naturally to writers of a certain temperament, and be put to fresh use; but the fact that their number is strictly limited is of interest; and suggests that the beam of light can only be manipulated in certain ways.

I will select, as a typical example, a recent book about a witch: *Flecker's Magic,* by Norman Matson.

It seemed to me good and I recommended it to a friend whose judgment I respect. He thought it poor. That is what is so tiresome about new books; they never give us that restful feeling which we have when perusing the classics. *Flecker's Magic* contains scarcely anything that is new—fantasies cannot: only the old old story of the wishing-ring which brings either misery or nothing at all. Flecker, an American boy who is learning to paint in Paris, is given the ring by a girl in a café; she is a witch, she tells him; he has only to be sure what he wants and he will get it. To prove her power, a motor-bus rises slowly from the street and turns upside down in the air. The passengers, who do not fall out, try to look as if nothing was happening. The driver, who is standing on the pavement at the moment, cannot conceal his surprise, but when his bus returns safe to earth again he thinks it wiser to get into his seat and drive off as usual. Motor-buses do not revolve slowly through the air—so they do not. Flecker now accepts the ring. His character, though slightly sketched, is individual, and this definiteness causes the book to grip.

It proceeds with a growing tension, a series of little shocks. The method is Socratic. The boy starts by thinking of something obvious, like a Rolls-Royce. But where shall he put the beastly thing? Or a beautiful lady. But what about her *carte d'identité*? Or money? Ah, that's more like it—he is almost a beggar. Say a million dollars. He prepares to turn the ring for this wish—except while one's about it two millions seem safer—or ten—or—and money blares out into madness, and the same thing happens when he thinks of long life: to die in forty years—no, in fifty—in one hundred—horrible, horrible. Then a solution occurs. He has always wanted to be a great painter. Well, he'll be it at once. But what kind of greatness? Giotto's? Cézanne's? Certainly not; his own kind, and he does not know what that is, so this wish likewise is impossible.

And now a horrible old woman begins to haunt his days and dreams. She reminds him vaguely of the girl who gave him the ring. She knows his thoughts and she is always sidling up to him in the streets and saying, "Dear boy—darling boy—wish for happiness." We learn in time that she is the real witch—the girl was a human acquaintance whom she used to get into touch with Flecker. The last of the witches—very lonely. The rest have committed suicide during the eighteenth century—they could not endure to survive into the world of Newton where two and two make four, and even the world of Einstein is not sufficiently decentralised to revive them. She has hung on in the hope of smashing this world, and she wants the boy to ask for happiness because such a wish has never been made in all the history of the ring.

Perhaps Flecker was the first modern man to find himself in this predicament? The people of the old world had so little they knew surely what they wanted. They knew about Almighty God, who wore a beard and sat in an armchair about a mile above the fields, and life was very short and very long too, for the days were so full of unthinking effort.

The people of the recorded olden times wished for a beautiful castle on a high hill and lived therein until death. But the hill was not so high one might see from the windows back along thirty centuries—as one may from a bungalow. In the castle there were no great volumes filled with words and pictures of things dug up by man's relentless curiosity from sand and soil in all corners of the world; there was a sentimental half-belief in dragons, but no knowledge that once upon a time only dragons had lived on the earth—that man's grandfather and grandmother were dragons; there were no movies flickering like thoughts against a white wall, no phonograph, no machinery with which to achieve the sensation of speed; no diagrams of the fourth dimension, no contrasts in life like that of Waterville, Minn., and Paris, France. In the castle the light was weak and flickering, hallways were dark, rooms deeply shadowed. The little outside world was full of shadow, and on the very top of the mind of him who lived in the castle played a dim light—underneath were shadows, fear, ignorance, will-to-ignorance. Most of all, there was not in the castle on the hill the breathless sense of imminent revelation—that today or surely tomorrow Man would at a stroke double his power and change the world again.

The ancient tales of magic were the mumbling thoughts of a distant shabby little world—so, at least, thought Flecker, offended. The tales gave him no guidance. There was too much difference between his world and theirs.

He wondered if he hadn't dismissed the wish for happiness rather heedlessly? He seemed to get nowhere thinking about it. He was not wise enough. In the old tales a wish for happiness was never made! He wondered why.

He might chance it—just to see what would happen. The thought made him tremble. He leaped from his bed and paced the red-tiled floor, rubbing his hands together. "I want to be happy for ever," he whispered, to hear the words, careful not to touch the ring. *"Happy . . . for ever"*—the two syllables of the first word, like hard little pebbles, struck musically against the bell of his imagination, but the second was a sigh. *For ever*—his spirit sank under the soft heavy impact of it. Held in his thought the word made a dreary music, fading. *"Happy for ever"* —NO! !

Thus again and again—the mark of the true fantasist—does Norman Matson merge the kingdoms of magic and comon sense by using words that apply to both, and the mixture he has created comes alive. I will not tell the end of the story. You will have guessed its essentials, but there are always surprises in the working of a fresh mind, and to the end of time good literature will be made round this notion of a wish.

To turn from this simple example of the supernatural to a more complicated one—to a highly accomplished and superbly written book whose spirit is farcical: *Zuleika Dobson* by Max Beerbohm. You all know Miss Dobson—not personally, or you would not be here now. She is that damsel for love of whom all the undergraduates of Oxford except one drowned themselves during Eights week, and he threw himself out of a window.

A superb theme for a fantasy, but all will depend on the handling. It is treated with a mixture of realism, wittiness, charm and mythology, and the mythology is most important. Max has borrowed or created a number of supernatural machines—to have entrusted Zuleika to one of them would be inept; the fantasy would become heavy or thin. But we pass from the sweating emperors to the black and pink pearls, the hooting owls, the interference of the muse Clio, the ghosts of Chopin and George Sand, of Nellie O'Mora; just as one fails another starts, to uphold this gayest and most exquisite of funeral palls.

Through the square, across the High, down Grove Street they passed. The Duke looked up at the tower of Merton, *ὣς οὔποτ' αὖθις ἀλλὰ νῦν πανύστατον.* Strange that tonight it would still be standing here, in all its sober and solid beauty—still be gazing, over the roofs and chimneys, at the tower of Magdalen, its rightful bride. Through untold centuries of the future it would stand thus, gaze thus. He winced. Oxford walls have a way of belittling us; and the Duke was loth to regard his doom as trivial.

Aye, by all minerals we are mocked. Vegetables, yearly deciduous, are far more sympathetic. The lilac and laburnum, making lovely now the railed pathway to Christ Church meadow, were all a-swaying and nodding to the Duke as he passed by. "Adieu, adieu, your Grace," they were whispering. "We are very sorry for you, very sorry indeed. We never dared suppose you would predecease us. We think your death a very great tragedy. Adieu! Perhaps we shall meet in another world—that is, if the members of the animal kingdom have immortal souls, as we have."

The Duke was little versed in their language; yet, as he passed between these gently garrulous blooms, he caught at the least the drift of their salutation, and smiled a vague but courteous acknowledgment, to the right and the left alternately, creating a very favourable impression.

Has not a passage like this—with its freedom of invocation—a beauty unattainable by serious literature? It is so funny and charming, so iridescent yet so profound. Criticisms of human nature fly through the book, not like arrows but upon the wings of sylphs. Towards the end—that dreadful end often so fatal to fiction—the book rather flags: the suicide of all the undergraduates of Oxford is not as delightful as it ought to be when viewed at close quarters, and the defenestration of Noaks almost nasty. Still it is a great work—the most consistent achievement of fantasy in our time, and the closing scene in Zuleika's bedroom with its menace of further disasters is impeccable.

And now with pent breath and fast-beating heart, she stared at the lady of the mirror, without seeing her; and now she wheeled round and swiftly glided to that little table on which stood her two books. She snatched Bradshaw.

We always intervene between Bradshaw and any one whom we see consulting him. "Mademoiselle will permit me to find that which she seeks?" asked Melisande.

"Be quiet," said Zuleika. We always repulse, at first, any one who intervenes between us and Bradshaw.

We always end by accepting the intervention. "See if it is possible to go direct from here to Cambridge," said Zuleika, handing the book on "If it isn't, then—well, see how one *does* get there."

We never have any confidence in the intervener. Nor is the intervener, when it comes to the point, sanguine.

With mistrust mounting to exasperation Zuleika sat watching the faint and frantic researches of her maid.

"Stop!" she said suddenly. "I have a much better idea. Go down very early to the station. See the station-master. Order me a special train. For ten o'clock, say."

Rising, she stretched her arms above her head. Her lips parted in a yawn, met in a smile. With both hands she pushed back her hair from her shoulders, and twisted it into a loose knot. Very lightly she slipped up into bed, and very soon she was asleep.

So Zuleika ought to have come on to this place. She does not seem ever to have arrived and we can only suppose that through the intervention of the gods her special train failed to start, or, more likely, is still in a siding at Bletchley.

Among the devices in my list I mentioned "parody" or "adaptation" and would now examine this further. The fantasist here adopts for his mythology some earlier work and uses it as a framework or quarry for his own purposes. There is an aborted example of this in *Joseph Andrews*. Fielding set out to use *Pamela* as a comic mythology. He thought it would be fun to invent a brother to Pamela, a pure-minded footman, who should repulse Lady Booby's attentions just as Pamela had repulsed Mr. B.'s, and he made Lady Booby Mr. B.'s aunt. Thus he would be able to laugh at Richardson, and incidentally express his own views of life. Fielding's view of life however was of the sort that only rests content with the creation of solid round characters, and with the growth of Parson Adams and Mrs. Slipslop the fantasy ceases, and we get an independent work. *Joseph*

Andrews (which is also important historically) is interesting to us as an example of a false start. Its author begins by playing the fool in a Richardsonian world, and ends by being serious in a world of his own—the world of Tom Jones and Amelia.

Parody or adaptation have enormous advantages to certain novelists, particularly to those who may have a great deal to say and plenty of literary genius, but who do not see the world in terms of individual men and women—who do not, in other words, take easily to creating characters. How are such men to start writing? An already existing book or literary tradition may inspire them—they may find high up in its cornices a pattern that will serve as a beginning, they may swing about in its rafters and gain strength. That fantasy of Lowes Dickinson, *The Magic Flute,* seems to be created thus: it has taken as its mythology the world of Mozart. Tamino, Sarastro, and the Queen of the Night stand in their enchanted kingdom ready for the author's thoughts, and when these are poured in they become alive and a new and exquisite work is born. And the same is true of another fantasy, anything but exquisite—James Joyce's *Ulysses.*[1] That remarkable affair—perhaps the most interesting literary experiment of our day—could not have been achieved unless Joyce had had, as his guide and butt, the world of the *Odyssey.*

[1] *Ulysses,* Shakespeare & Co., Paris, is not at present obtainable in England. America, more enlightened, has produced a mutilated version without the author's permission and without paying him a cent.

I am only touching on one aspect of *Ulysses*: it is of course more than a fantasy—it is a dogged attempt to cover the universe with mud, it is an inverted Victorianism, an attempt to make crossness and dirt succeed where sweetness and light failed, a simplification of the human character in the interests of Hell. All simplifications are fascinating, all lead us away from the truth (which lies far nearer the muddle of *Tristram Shandy*), and *Ulysses* must not detain us on the ground that it contains a morality—otherwise we shall also have to discuss Mrs. Humphry Ward. We are concerned with it because, through a mythology, Joyce has been able to create the peculiar stage and characters he required.

The action of those 400,000 words occupies a single day, the scene is Dublin, the theme is a journey—the modern man's journey from morn to midnight, from bed to the squalid tasks of mediocrity, to a funeral, newspaper office, library, pub, lavatory, lying-in hospital, a saunter by the beach, brothel, coffee stall, and so back to bed. And it coheres because it depends from the journey of a hero through the seas of Greece, like a bat hanging to a cornice.

Ulysses himself is Mr. Leopold Bloom—a converted Jew—greedy, lascivious, timid, undignified, desultory, superficial, kindly and always at his lowest when he pretends to aspire. He tries to explore life through the body. Penelope is Mrs. Marion Bloom, an overblown soprano, by no means harsh to her suitors. The third character is young Stephen Dedalus, whom Bloom recognizes as his spiritual son much as Ulysses recognizes Telemachus as his actual son. Stephen tries to explore life through the intellect—we have met him before in *The Portrait of the Artist as a Young Man,* and now he is worked into this epic of grubbiness and disillusion. He and Bloom meet half-way through in Night Town (which corresponds partly to Homer's Palace of Circe, partly to his Descent into Hell) and in its supernatural and filthy alleys they strike up their slight but genuine friendship. This is the crisis of the book, and here—and indeed throughout—smaller mythologies swarm and pullulate, like vermin between the scales of a poisonous snake. Heaven and earth fill with infernal life, personalities melt, sexes interchange, until the whole universe, including poor, pleasure-loving Mr. Bloom, is involved in one joyless orgy.

Does it come off? No, not quite. Indignation in literature never quite comes off either in Juvenal or Swift or Joyce; there is something in words that is alien to its simplicity. The Night Town scene does not come off except as a superfetation of fantasies, a monstrous coupling of reminiscences. Such satisfaction as can be attained in this direction is attained, and all through the book we have similar experiments—the aim of which is to degrade all things and more particularly civilization and art, by turning them inside out and upside down. Some enthusiasts may think that *Ulysses* ought to be mentioned not here but later on, under the heading of prophecy, and I understand this criticism. But I prefer to mention it today with *Tristram Shandy,*

Flecker's Magic, Zuleika Dobson, and *The Magic Flute,* because the raging of Joyce, like the happier or calmer moods of the other writers, seems essentially fantastic, and lacks the note for which we shall be listening soon.

We must pursue this notion of mythology further and more circumspectly.

Seven

PROPHECY

WITH prophecy in the narrow sense of foretelling the future we have no concern, and we have not much concern with it as an appeal for righteousness. What will interest us today—what we must respond to, for interest now becomes an inappropriate word—is an accent in the novelist's voice, an accent for which the flutes and saxophones of fantasy may have prepared us. His theme is the universe, or something universal, but he is not necessarily going to "say" anything about the universe; he proposes to sing, and the strangeness of song arising in the halls of fiction is bound to give us a shock. How will song combine with the furniture of common sense? we shall ask ourselves, and shall have to answer "not too well": the singer does not always have room for his gestures, the tables and chairs get broken, and the novel through which bardic influence has passed often has a wrecked air, like a drawing-room after an earthquake or a children's party. Readers of D. H. Lawrence will understand what I mean.

Prophecy—in our sense—is a tone of voice. It may imply any of the faiths that have haunted humanity

—Christianity, Buddhism, dualism, Satanism, or the mere raising of human love and hatred to such a power that their normal receptacles no longer contain them: but what particular view of the universe is recommended—with that we are not directly concerned. It is the implication that signifies and will filter into the turns of the novelist's phrase, and in this lecture, which promises to be so vague and grandiose, we may come nearer than elsewhere to the minutiae of style. We shall have to attend to the novelist's state of mind and to the actual words he uses; we shall neglect as far as we can the problems of common sense. As far as we can: for all novels contain tables and chairs, and most readers of fiction look for them first. Before we condemn him for affectation and distortion we must realize his view-point. He is not looking at the tables and chairs at all, and that is why they are out of focus. We only see what he does not focus—not what he does—and in our blindness we laugh at him.

I have said that each aspect of the novel demands a different quality in the reader. Well, the prophetic aspect demands two qualities: humility and the suspension of the sense of humour. Humility is a quality for which I have only a limited admiration. In many phases of life it is a great mistake and degenerates into defensiveness or hypocrisy. But humility is in place just now. Without its help we shall not hear the voice of the prophet, and our eyes will behold a figure of fun instead of his glory. And the sense of humour—that is out of place: that estimable adjunct of the educated man must be laid aside. Like the schoolchildren in the Bible, one cannot help laughing at a prophet—his bald head is so absurd—but one can discount the laughter and realize that it has no critical value and is merely food for bears.

Let us distinguish between the prophet and the non-prophet.

There were two novelists, who were both brought up in Christianity. They speculated and broke away, yet they neither left nor did they want to leave the Christian spirit which they interpreted as a loving spirit. They both held that sin is always punished, and punishment a purgation, and they saw this process not with the detachment of an ancient Greek or a modern Hindu, but with tears in their eyes. Pity, they felt, is the atmosphere in which morality exercises its logic, a logic which otherwise is crude and meaningless. What is the use of a sinner being punished and cured if there is not an addition in the cure, a heavenly bonus? And where does the addition come from? Not out of the machinery, but out of the atmosphere in which the process occurs, out of the love and pity which (they believed) are attributes of God.

How similar these two novelists must have been! Yet one of them was George Eliot and the other Dostoevsky.

It will be said that Dostoevsky had vision. Still, so had George Eliot. To classify them apart—and they must be parted—is not so easy. But the difference between them will define itself at once exactly if I read two passages from their works. To the classifier the passages will seem similar: to anyone who has an ear for song they come out of different worlds.

I will begin with a passage—fifty years ago it was a very famous passage—out of *Adam Bede*. Hetty is in prison, condemned to die for the murder of her illegitimate child. She will not confess, she is hard and impenitent. Dinah, the Methodist, comes to visit her and tries to touch her heart.

> Dinah began to doubt whether Hetty was conscious who it was that sat beside her. But she felt the Divine presence more and more—nay, as if she herself were a part of it, and it was the Divine pity that was beating in her heart, and was willing the rescue of this helpless one. At last she was prompted to speak, and find out how far Hetty was conscious of the present.
>
> "Hetty," she said gently, "do you know who it is that sits by your side?"
>
> "Yes," Hetty answered slowly, "it's Dinah." Then, after a pause, she added, "But you can do nothing for me. You can't make 'em do anything. They'll hang me o' Monday—it's Friday now."
>
> "But, Hetty, there is some one else in this cell besides me, some one close to you."
>
> Hetty said, in a frightened whisper, "Who?"
>
> "Some one who has been with you through all your hours of sin and trouble—who has known every thought you have had—has seen where you went, where you lay down and rose up again, and all the deeds you have tried to hide in darkness. And on Monday, when I can't follow you, when my arms can't reach you, when death has parted us, He who is with you now and knows all, will

be with you then. It makes no difference—whether we live or die we are in the presence of God."

"Oh, Dinah, won't nobody do anything for me? *Will* they hang me for certain? . . . I wouldn't mind if they'd let me live . . . help me. . . . I can't feel anything like you . . . my heart is hard."

Dinah held the clinging hand, and all her soul went forth in her voice: ". . . Come, mighty Saviour! let the dead hear Thy voice; let the eyes of the blind be opened: let her see that God encompasses her; let her tremble at nothing but the sin that cuts her off from Him. Melt the hard heart; unseal the closed lips: make her cry with her whole soul, 'Father, I have sinned.' "

"Dinah," Hetty sobbed out, throwing her arms round Dinah's neck, "I will speak . . . I will tell . . . I won't hide it any more. I did do it, Dinah . . . I buried in the wood . . . the little baby . . . and it cried . . . I heard it cry . . . ever such a way off . . . all night . . . and I went back because it cried."

She paused and then spoke hurriedly in a louder pleading tone.

"But I thought perhaps it wouldn't die—there might somebody find it. I didn't kill it—I didn't kill it myself. I put it down there and covered it up, and when I came back it was gone. . . . I don't know what I felt until I found that the baby was gone. And when I put it there, I thought I should like somebody to find it and save it from dying, but when I saw it was gone, I was struck like a stone, with fear. I never thought o' stirring, I felt so weak. I knew I couldn't run away, and everybody as saw me 'ud know about the baby. My heart went like stone; I couldn't wish or try for anything; it seemed like as if I should stay there for ever, and nothing 'ud ever change. But they came and took me away."

Hetty was silent, but she shuddered again, as if there

was still something behind: and Dinah waited, for her heart was so full that tears must come before words. At last Hetty burst out with a sob,

"Dinah, do you think God will take away that crying and the place in the wood, now I've told everything?"

"Let us pray, poor sinner: let us fall on our knees again, and pray to the God of all mercy."

I have not done justice to this scene, because I have had to cut it, and it is on her massiveness that George Eliot depends—she has no nicety of style. The scene is sincere, solid, pathetic, and penetrated with Christianity. The god whom Dinah summons is a living force to the authoress also: he is not brought in to work up the reader's feelings; he is the natural accompaniment of human error and suffering.

Now contrast with it the following scene from *The Brothers Karamazov* (Mitya is being accused of the murder of his father, of which he is indeed spiritually though not technically guilty).

They proceeded to a final revision of the protocol. Mitya got up, moved from his chair to the corner by the curtain, lay down on a large chest covered by a rug, and instantly fell asleep.

He had a strange dream, utterly out of keeping with the place and the time.

He was driving somewhere in the steppes, where he had been stationed long ago, and a peasant was driving him in a cart with a pair of horses, through snow and sleet. Not far off was a village; he could see the black huts, and half the huts were burned down, there were only the charred beams sticking up. And as they drove in, there were peasant women drawn up along the road, a lot of women, a whole row, all thin and wan, with their faces a sort of brownish colour, especially one at the edge, a tall bony woman, who looked forty, but might have been only twenty, with a long thin face. And in her arms was a little baby crying. And her breasts seemed so dried up that there was not a drop of milk in them. And the child cried and cried, and held out its little bare arms, with its little fists blue from cold.

"Why are they crying? Why are they crying?" Mitya asked as they dashed gaily by.

"It's the babe," answered the driver. "The babe weeping."

And Mitya was struck by his saying, in his peasant way, "the babe," and he liked the peasant calling it "the babe." There seemed more pity in it.

"But why is it weeping?" Mitya persisted stupidly. "Why are its little arms bare? Why don't they wrap it up?"

"Why they're poor people, burnt out. They've no bread. They're begging because they've been burnt out."

"No, no," Mitya, as it were, still did not understand. "Tell me, why is it those poor mothers stand there? Why are people poor? Why is the babe poor? Why is the steppe barren? Why don't they hug each other and kiss? Why don't they sing songs of joy? Why are they so dark from black misery? Why don't they feed the babe?"

And he felt that, though his questions were unreasonable and senseless, yet he wanted to ask just that, and he had to ask it just in that way. And he felt that a passion of pity, such as he had never known before, was rising in his heart, that he wanted to cry, that he wanted to do something for them all, so that the babe should weep no more, so that the dark-faced dried-up mother should not weep, that no one should shed tears again from that moment, and he wanted to do it at once, at once, regardless of all obstacles, with all the recklessness of the Karamazovs. . . . And his heart glowed, and he struggled forward towards the light, and he longed to live, to go on and on, towards the new beckoning light, and to hasten, hasten, now, at once!

"What! Where?" he exclaimed, opening his eyes, and sitting up on the chest, as though he had revived from a swoon, smiling brightly. Nikolay Parfenovitch was standing over him, suggesting that he should hear the protocol read aloud and sign it. Mitya guessed that he had been asleep an hour or more, but he did not hear Nikolay Parfenovitch. He was suddenly struck by the fact that there was a pillow under his head, which hadn't been there when he leant back exhausted, on the chest.

"Who put that pillow under my head? Who was so kind?" he cried, with a sort of ecstatic gratitude, and tears in his voice, as though some great kindness had been shown him.

He never found out who this kind man was, perhaps one of the peasant witnesses, or Nikolay Parfenovitch's little secretary had compassionately thought to put a pillow under his head, but his whole soul was quivering with tears. He went to the table and said he would sign whatever they liked.

"I've had a good dream, gentlemen," he said in a strange voice, with a new light, as of joy, in his face.

Now what is the difference in these passages—a difference that throbs in every phrase? It is that the first writer is a preacher, and the second a prophet. George Eliot talks about God, but never alters her focus; God and the tables and chairs are all in the same plane, and in consequence we have not for a moment the feeling that the whole universe needs pity and love—they are only needed in Hetty's cell. In Dostoevsky the characters and situations always stand for more than themselves; infinity attends them; though yet they remain individuals they expand to embrace it and summon it to embrace them; one can apply to them the saying of St. Catherine of Siena that God is in the soul and the soul is in God as the sea is in the fish and the fish is in the sea. Every sentence he writes implies this extension, and the implication is the dominant aspect of his work. He is a great novelist in the ordinary sense—that is to say his characters have relation to ordinary life and also live in their own surroundings, there are incidents which keep us excited, and so on; he has also the greatness of a prophet, to which our ordinary standards are inapplicable.

That is the gulf between Hetty and Mitya, though they inhabit the same moral and mythological worlds. Hetty, taken by herself, is quite adequate. She is a poor girl, brought to confess her crime, and so to a better frame of mind. But Mitya, taken by himself, is not adequate. He only becomes real through what he implies, his mind is not in a frame at all. Taken by himself he seems distorted out of drawing, intermittent; we begin explaining him away and saying he was disproportionately grateful for the pillow because he was overwrought—very like a Russian in fact. We cannot understand him until we see that he extends, and that the part of him on which Dostoevsky focused did not lie on that wooden chest or even in dreamland but in a region where it could be joined by the rest of humanity. Mitya is—all of us. So is Alyosha, so is Smerdyakov. He is the prophetic vision, and the novelist's creation also. He does not become all of us here: he is Mitya here as Hetty is Hetty. The extension, the melting, the unity through love and pity occur in a region which can only be implied and to which fiction is perhaps the wrong approach. The world of the Karamazovs and Myshkin and Raskolnikov, the world of Moby Dick which we shall enter shortly, it is not a veil, it is not an allegory. It is the ordinary world of fiction, but it reaches back. And that tiny humorous figure of Lady Bertram whom we considered some time ago—Lady Bertram sitting on her sofa with pug—may assist us in these deeper matters. Lady Bertram, we decided, was a flat character, capable of extending into a round when the action required it. Mitya is a round character, but he is capable of extension. He does not conceal anything (mysticism), he does not mean anything (symbolism), he is merely Dmitri Karamazov, but to be merely a person in Dostoevsky is to join up with all the other people far back. Consequently the tremendous current suddenly flows—for me in those closing words: "I've had a good dream, gentlemen." Have I had that good dream too? No, Dostoevsky's characters ask us to share something deeper than their experiences. They convey to us a sensation that is partly physical—the sensation of sinking into a translucent globe and seeing our experience floating far above us on its surface, tiny, remote, yet ours. We have not ceased to be people, we have given nothing up, but "the sea is in the fish and the fish is in the sea."

There we touch the limit of our subject. We are

not concerned with the prophet's message, or rather (since matter and manner cannot be wholly separated) we are concerned with it as little as possible. What matters is the accent of his voice, his song. Hetty might have a good dream in prison, and it would be true of her, satisfyingly true, but it would stop short. Dinah would say she was glad, Hetty would recount her dream, which, unlike Mitya's, would be logically connected with the crisis, and George Eliot would say something sound and sympathetic about good dreams generally, and their inexplicably helpful effect on the tortured breast. Just the same and absolutely different are the two scenes, the two books, the two writers.

Now another point appears. Regarded merely as a novelist the prophet has certain uncanny advantages, so that it is sometimes worth letting him into a drawing-room even on the furniture's account. Perhaps he will smash or distort, but perhaps he will illumine. As I said of the fantasist, he manipulates a beam of light which occasionally touches the objects so sedulously dusted by the hand of common sense, and renders them more vivid than they can ever be in domesticity. This intermittent realism pervades all the greater works of Dostoevsky and Herman Melville. Dostoevsky can be patiently accurate about a trial or the appearance of a staircase. Melville can catalogue the products of the whale ("I have ever found the plain things the knottiest of all," he remarks). D. H. Lawrence can describe a field of grass and flowers or the entrance into Fremantle. Little things in the foreground seem to be all that the prophet cares about at moments—he sits down with them so quiet and busy like a child between two romps. What does he feel during these intermittencies? Is it another form of excitement, or is he resting? We cannot know. No doubt it is what A.E. feels when he is doing his creameries, or what Claudel feels when he is doing his diplomacy, but what is that? Anyhow, it characterizes these novels and gives them what is always provocative in a work of art: roughness of surface. While they pass under our eyes they are full of dents and grooves and lumps and spikes which draw from us little cries of approval and disapproval. When they have past, the roughness is forgotten, they become as smooth as the moon.

Prophetic fiction, then, seems to have definite characteristics. It demands humility and the absence of the sense of humour. It reaches back—though we must not conclude from the example of Dostoevsky that it always reaches back to pity and love. It is spasmodically realistic. And it gives us the sensation of a song or of sound. It is unlike fantasy because its face is towards unity, whereas fantasy glances about. Its confusion is incidental, whereas fantasy's is fundamental—*Tristram Shandy* ought to be a muddle, *Zuleika Dobson* ought to keep changing mythologies. Also the prophet—one imagines—has gone "off" more completely than the fantasist, he is in a remoter emotional state while he composes. Not many novelists have this aspect. Poe is too incidental. Hawthorne potters too anxiously round the problem of individual salvation to get free. Hardy, a philosopher and a great poet, might seem to have claims, but Hardy's novels are surveys, they do not give out sounds. The writer sits back, it is true, but the characters do not reach back. He shows them to us as they let their arms rise and fall in the air; they may parallel our sufferings but can never extend them—never, I mean, could Jude step forward like Mitya and release floods of our emotion by saying "Gentlemen, I've had a bad dream." Conrad is in a rather similar position. The voice, the voice of Marlow, is too full of experiences to sing, it is dulled by many reminiscences of error and beauty, its owner has seen too much to see beyond cause and effect. To have a philosophy—even a poetic and emotional philosophy like Hardy's and Conrad's—leads to reflections on life and things. A prophet does not reflect. And he does not hammer away. That is why we exclude Joyce. Joyce has many qualities akin to prophecy and he has shown (especially in the *Portrait of the Artist*) an imaginative grasp of evil. But he undermines the universe in too workmanlike a manner, looking round for this tool or that: in spite of all his internal looseness he is too tight, he is never vague except after due deliberation; it is talk, talk, never song.

So, though I believe this lecture is on a genuine aspect of the novel, not a fake aspect, I can only think of four writers to illustrate it—Dostoevsky, Melville, D. H. Lawrence and Emily Brontë. Emily

Brontë shall be left to the last, Dostoevsky I have alluded to, Melville is the centre of our picture, and the centre of Melville is *Moby Dick*.

Moby Dick is an easy book, as long as we read it as a yarn or an account of whaling interspersed with snatches of poetry. But as soon as we catch the song in it, it grows difficult and immensely important. Narrowed and hardened into words the spiritual theme of *Moby Dick* is as follows: a battle against evil conducted too long or in the wrong way. The White Whale is evil, and Captain Ahab is warped by constant pursuit until his knight-errantry turns into revenge. These are words—a symbol for the book if we want one—but they do not carry us much further than the acceptance of the book as a yarn—perhaps they carry us backwards, for they may mislead us into harmonizing the incidents, and so losing their roughness and richness. The idea of a contest we may retain: all action is a battle, the only happiness is peace. But contest between what? We get false if we say that it is between good and evil or between two unreconciled evils. The essential in *Moby Dick*, its prophetic song, flows athwart the action and the surface morality like an undercurrent. It lies outside words. Even at the end, when the ship has gone down with the bird of heaven pinned to its mast, and the empty coffin, bouncing up from the vortex, has carried Ishmael back to the world—even then we cannot catch the words of the song. There has been stress, with intervals: but no explicable solution, certainly no reaching back into universal pity and love; no "Gentlemen, I've had a good dream."

The extraordinary nature of the book appears in two of its early incidents—the sermon about Jonah and the friendship with Queequeg.

The sermon has nothing to do with Christianity. It asks for endurance or loyalty without hope of reward. The preacher "kneeling in the pulpit's bows, folded his large brown hands across his chest, uplifted his closed eyes, and offered a prayer so deeply devout that he seemed kneeling and praying at the bottom of the sea." Then he works up and up and concludes on a note of joy that is far more terrifying than a menace.

> Delight is to him whose strong arms yet support him when the ship of this base treacherous world has gone down beneath him. Delight is to him who gives no quarter in the truth, and kills, burns and destroys all sin though he pluck it out from under the robes of Senators and Judges. Delight—top-gallant delight is to him, who acknowledges no law or lord, but the Lord his God, and is onry a patriot to heaven. Delight is to him, whom all the waves of the billows of the seas of the boisterous mob can never shake from this sure Keel of the Ages. And eternal delight and deliciousness will be his, who coming to lay him down, can say with his final breath—O Father!—chiefly known to me by thy rod—mortal or immortal, here I die. I have striven to be Thine, more than to be this world's or mine own. Yet this is nothing: I leave eternity to Thee: for what is man that he should live out the lifetime of his God?

I believe it is not a coincidence that the last ship we encounter at the end of the book before the final catastrophe should be called the Delight; a vessel of ill omen who has herself encountered Moby Dick and been shattered by him. But what the connection was in the prophet's mind I cannot say, nor could he tell us.

Immediately after the sermon, Ishmael makes a passionate alliance with the cannibal Queequeg, and it looks for a moment that the book is to be a saga of blood-brotherhood. But human relationships mean little to Melville, and after a grotesque and violent entry, Queequeg is almost forgotten. Almost —not quite. Towards the end he falls ill and a coffin is made for him which he does not occupy, as he recovers. It is this coffin, serving as a life-buoy, that saves Ishmael from the final whirlpool, and this again is no coincidence, but an unformulated connection that sprang up in Melville's mind. *Moby Dick* is full of meanings: its meaning is a different problem. It is wrong to turn the Delight or the coffin into symbols, because even if the symbolism is correct, it silences the book. Nothing can be stated about *Moby Dick* except that it is a contest. The rest is song.

It is to his conception of evil that Melville's work owes much of its strength. As a rule evil has been feebly envisaged in fiction, which seldom soars above misconduct or avoids the clouds of mysteriousness. Evil to most novelists is either sexual and social or is something very vague for which a special style with implications of poetry is thought suitable. They want it to exist, in order that it may kindly help them on with the plot, and evil, not being kind, generally hampers them with a villain—a Lovelace or Uriah Heep, who does more harm to the author than to the fellow characters. For a real villain we must turn to a story of Melville's called *Billy Budd.*[1]

It is a short story, but must be mentioned because of the light it throws on his other work. The scene is on a British man-of-war soon after the Mutiny at the Nore—a stagey yet intensely real vessel. The hero, a young sailor, has goodness—which is faint beside the goodness of Alyosha; still he has goodness of the glowing aggressive sort which cannot exist unless it has evil to consume. He is not aggressive himself. It is the light within him that irritates and explodes. On the surface he is a pleasant, merry, rather insensitive lad, whose perfect physique is marred by one slight defect, a stammer, which finally destroys him. He is "dropped into a world not without some man-traps, and against whose subtleties simple courage without any touch of defensive ugliness is of little avail; and where such innocence as man is capable of does yet, in a moral emergency, not always sharpen the faculties or enlighten the will." Claggart, one of the petty officers, at once sees in him the enemy—his own enemy, for Claggart is evil. It is again the contest between Ahab and

[1] Only to be found in a collected edition. For knowledge of it, and for much else, I am indebted to Mr. John Freeman's admirable monograph on Melville.

Moby Dick, though the parts are more clearly assigned, and we are further from prophecy and nearer to morality and common sense. But not much nearer. Claggart is not like any other villain.

> Naturally depravity has certain negative virtues, serving it as silent auxiliaries. It is not going too far to say that it is without vices or small sins. There is a phenomenal pride in it that excludes them from anything—never mercenary or avaricious. In short, the character here meant partakes nothing of the sordid or sensual. It is serious, but free from acerbity.

He accuses Billy of trying to foment a mutiny. The charge is ridiculous, no one believes it, and yet it proves fatal. For when the boy is summoned to declare his innocence, he is so horrified that he cannot speak, his ludicrous stammer seizes him, the power within him explodes, and he knocks down his traducer, kills him, and has to be hanged.

Billy Budd is a remote unearthly episode, but it is a song not without words, and should be read both for its own beauty and as an introduction to more difficult works. Evil is labelled and personified instead of slipping over the ocean and round the world, and Melville's mind can be observed more easily. What one notices in him is that his apprehensions are free from personal worry, so that we become bigger not smaller after sharing them. He has not got that tiresome little receptacle, a conscience, which is often such a nuisance in serious writers and so contracts their effects—the conscience of Hawthorne or of Mark Rutherford. Melville—after the initial roughness of his realism—reaches straight back into the universal, to a blackness and sadness so transcending our own that they are undistinguishable from glory. He says, "in certain moods no man can weigh this world without throwing in a something somehow like Original Sin to strike the uneven balance." He threw it in, that undefinable something, the balance righted itself, and he gave us harmony and temporary salvation.

It is no wonder that D. H. Lawrence should have written two penetrating studies of Melville, for Lawrence himself is, as far as I know, the only prophetic novelist writing today—all the rest are fantasists or preachers: the only living novelist in whom the song predominates, who has the rapt bardic quality, and whom it is idle to criticize. He invites criticism because he is a preacher also—it is this minor aspect of him which makes him so difficult and misleading—an excessively clever preacher who knows how to play on the nerves of his congregation. Nothing is more disconcerting than to sit down, so to speak, before your prophet, and then suddenly to receive his boot in the pit of your stomach. "I'm damned if I'll be humble after that," you cry, and so lay yourself open to further nagging. Also the subject matter of the sermon is agitating—hot denunciations or advice—so that in the end you cannot remember whether you ought or ought not to have a body, and are only sure that you are futile. This bullying, and the honeyed sweetness which is a bully's reaction, occupy between them the foreground of Lawrence's work;

his greatness lies far, far back, and rests, not like Dostoevsky's upon Christianity, nor like Melville's upon a contest, but upon something aesthetic. The voice is Balder's voice, though the hands are the hands of Esau. The prophet is irradiating nature from within, so that every colour has a glow and every form a distinctness which could not otherwise be obtained. Take a scene that always stays in the memory: that scene in *Women in Love* where one of the characters throws stones into the water at night to shatter the image of the moon. Why he throws, what the scene symbolizes, is unimportant. But the writer could not get such a moon and water otherwise; he reaches them by his special path which stamps them as more wonderful than any we can imagine. It is the prophet back where he started from, back where the rest of us are waiting by the edge of the pool, but with a power of re-creation and evocation we shall never possess.

Humility is not easy with this irritable and irritating author, for the humbler we get, the crosser he gets. Yet I do not see how else to read him. If we start resenting or mocking, his treasure disappears as surely as if we started obeying him. What is valuable about him cannot be put into words; it is colour, gesture and outline in people and things, the usual stock-in-trade of the novelist, but evolved by such a different process that they belong to a new world.

But what about Emily Brontë? Why should *Wuthering Heights* come into this inquiry? It is a story about human beings, it contains no view of the universe.

My answer is that the emotions of Heathcliffe and Catherine Earnshaw function differently to other emotions in fiction. Instead of inhabiting the characters, they surround them like thunder clouds, and generate the explosions that fill the novel from the moment when Lockwood dreams of the hand at the window down to the moment when Heathcliffe, with the same window open, is discovered dead. *Wuthering Heights* is filled with sound—storm and rushing wind—a sound more important than words and thoughts. Great as the novel is, one cannot afterwards remember anything in it but Heathcliffe and the elder Catherine. They cause the action by their separation: they close it by their union after death. No wonder they "walk"; what else could such beings do? Even when they were alive their love and hate transcended them.

Emily Brontë had in some ways a literal and careful mind. She constructed her novel on a time chart even more elaborate than Miss Austen's, and she arranged the Linton and Earnshaw families symmetrically, and she had a clear idea of the various legal steps by which Heathcliffe gained possession of their two properties.[1] Then why did she deliberately introduce muddle, chaos, tempest? Because in our sense of the word she was a prophetess: because what

[1] See that sound and brilliant essay, *The Structure of Wuthering Heights*, by C.P.S., Hogarth Press.

is implied is more important to her than what is said; and only in confusion could the figures of Heathcliffe and Catherine externalize their passion till it streamed through the house and over the moors. *Wuthering Heights* has no mythology beyond what these two characters provide: no great book is more cut off from the universals of Heaven and Hell. It is local, like the spirits it engenders, and whereas we may meet Moby Dick in any pond, we shall only encounter them among the harebells and limestone of their own county.

A concluding remark. Always, at the back of my mind, there lurks a reservation about this prophetic stuff, a reservation which some will make more strongly while others will not make it at all. Fantasy has asked us to pay something extra; and now prophecy asks for humility and even for a suspension of the sense of humour, so that we are not allowed to snigger when a tragedy is called *Billy Budd.* We have indeed to lay aside the single vision which we bring to most of literature and life and have been trying to use through most of our inquiry, and take up a different set of tools. Is this right? Another prophet, Blake, had no doubt that it was right.

May God us keep
From single vision and Newton's sleep,

he cried and he has painted that same Newton with a pair of compasses in his hand, describing a miserable mathematical triangle, and turning his back upon the gorgeous and immeasurable water growths of *Moby Dick*. Few will agree with Blake. Fewer will agree with Blake's Newton. Most of us will be eclectics to this side or that according to our temperament. The human mind is not a dignified organ, and I do not see how we can exercise it sincerely except through eclecticism. And the only advice I would offer my fellow eclectics is: "Do not be proud of your inconsistency. It is a pity, it is a pity that we should be equipped like this. It is a pity that Man cannot be at the same time impressive and truthful." For the first five lectures of this course we have used more or less the same set of tools. This time and last we have had to lay them down. Next time we shall take them up again, but with no certainty that they are the best equipment for a critic or that there is such a thing as a critical equipment.

Eight

PATTERN AND RHYTHM

OUR interludes, gay and grave, are over, and we return to the general scheme of the course. We began with the story, and having considered human beings, we proceeded to the plot which springs out of the story. Now we must consider something which springs mainly out of the plot, and to which the characters and any other element present also contribute. For this new aspect there appears to be no literary word—indeed the more the arts develop the more they depend on each other for definition. We will borrow from painting first and call it the pattern. Later we will borrow from music and call it rhythm. Unfortunately both these words are vague —when people apply rhythm or pattern to literature they are apt not to say what they mean and not to finish their sentences: it is, "Oh, but surely the rhythm . . ." or "Oh, but if you call that pattern . . ."

Before I discuss what pattern entails, and what qualities a reader must bring to its appreciation, I will give two examples of books with patterns so definite that a pictorial image sums them up: a book the shape of an hour-glass and a book the shape of a grand chain in that old-time dance, the Lancers.

Thais by Anatole France is the shape of an hour-glass.

There are two chief characters, Paphnuce the ascetic, Thais the courtesan. Paphnuce lives in the desert, he is saved and happy when the book starts. Thais leads a life of sin in Alexandria, and it is his duty to save her. In the central scene of the book they approach, he succeeds; she goes into a monastery and gains salvation, because she has met him, but he, because he has met her, is damned. The two characters converge, cross, and recede with mathematical precision, and part of the pleasure we get from the book is due to this. Such is the pattern of *Thais*—so simple that it makes a good starting-point for a difficult survey. It is the same as the story of *Thais,* when events unroll in their time-sequence, and the same as the plot of *Thais,* when we see the two characters bound by their previous actions and taking fatal steps whose consequence they do not see. But whereas the story appeals to our curiosity and the plot to our intelligence, the pattern appeals to our aesthetic sense, it causes us to see the book as a whole. We do not see it as an hour-glass—that is the hard jargon of the lecture room which must never be taken literally at this advanced stage of our inquiry. We just have a pleasure without knowing why, and when the pleasure is past, as it is now, and our minds are left free to explain it, a geometrical simile such as an hour-glass will be found helpful. If it was not for this hour-glass the story, the plot, and the characters of Thais and Paphnuce would none of them exert their full force, they would none of them breathe as they do. "Pattern," which seems so rigid, is connected with atmosphere, which seems so fluid.

Now for the book that is shaped like the grand chain: *Roman Pictures* by Percy Lubbock.

Roman Pictures is a social comedy. The narrator is a tourist in Rome; he there meets a kindly and shoddy friend of his, Deering, who rebukes him superciliously for staring at churches and sets him out to explore society. This he does, demurely obedient; one person hands him on to another; café, studio, Vatican and Quirinal purlieus are all reached, until finally, at the extreme end of his career he thinks, in a most aristocratic and dilapidated palazzo, whom should he meet but the second-rate Deering; Deering is his hostess's nephew, but had concealed it owing to some backfire of snobbery. The circle is complete, the original partners have rejoined, and greet one another with mutual confusion which turns to mild laughter.

What is so good in *Roman Pictures* is not the presence of the "grand chain" pattern—anyone can organize a grand chain—but the suitability of the pattern to the author's mood. Lubbock works all through by administering a series of little shocks, and by extending to his characters an elaborate charity which causes them to appear in a rather worse light than if no charity was wasted on them at all. It is the comic atmosphere, but sub-acid, meticulously benign. And at the end we discover to our delight that the atmosphere has been externalized, and that the partners, as they click together in the marchesa's drawing-room, have done the exact thing which the book requires, which it required from the start, and have bound the scattered incidents together with a thread woven out of their own substance.

Thais and *Roman Pictures* provide easy examples of pattern; it is not often that one can compare a book to a pictorial object with any accuracy, though curves, etc., are freely spoken of by critics who do not quite know what they want to say. We can only say (so far) that pattern is an aesthetic aspect of the novel, and that though it may be nourished by anything in the novel—any character, scene, word—it draws most of its nourishment from the plot. We noted, when discussing the plot, that it added to itself the quality of beauty; beauty a little surprised at her own arrival: that upon its neat carpentry there could be seen, by those who cared to see, the figure of the Muse; that Logic, at the moment of finishing its own house, laid the foundation of a new one. Here, here is the point where the aspect called pattern is most closely in touch with its material; here is our starting point. It springs mainly from the plot, accompanies it like a light in the clouds, and remains visible after it has departed. Beauty is sometimes the shape of the book, the book as a whole, the unity, and our examination would be easier if it was always this. But sometimes it is not. When it is not I shall call it rhythm. For the moment we are concerned with pattern only.

Let us examine at some length another book of the rigid type, a book with a unity, and in this sense an easy book, although it is by Henry James. We shall see in it pattern triumphant, and we shall also be able to see the sacrifices an author must make if he wants his pattern and nothing else to triumph.

The Ambassadors, like *Thais,* is the shape of an hour-glass. Strether and Chad, like Paphnuce and Thais, change places, and it is the realization of this that makes the book so satisfying at the close. The plot is elaborate and subtle, and proceeds by action or conversation or meditation through every paragraph. Everything is planned, everything fits; none of the minor characters are just decorative like the talkative Alexandrians at Nicias' banquet; they elaborate on the main theme, they work. The final effect is pre-arranged, dawns gradually on the reader, and is completely successful when it comes. Details of intrigue, of the various missions from America, may be forgotten, but the symmetry they have created is enduring.

Let us trace the growth of this symmetry.[1]

Strether, a sensitive middle-aged American, is commissioned by his old friend, Mrs. Newsome, whom he hopes to marry, to go to Paris and rescue her son Chad, who has gone to the bad in that ap-

[1] There is a masterly analysis of *The Ambassadors* from another standpoint in *The Craft of Fiction.*

propriate city. The Newsomes are sound commercial people, who have made money over manufacturing a small article of domestic utility. Henry James never tells us what the small article is, and in a moment we shall understand why. Wells spits it out in *Tono Bungay,* Meredith reels it out in *Evan Harrington,* Trollope prescribes it freely for Miss Dunstable, but for James to indicate how his characters made their pile—it would not do. The article is somewhat ignoble and ludicrous—that is enough. If you choose to be coarse and daring and visualize it for yourself as, say, a button-hook, you can, but you do so at your own risk: the author remains uninvolved.

Well, whatever it is, Chad Newsome ought to come back and help make it, and Strether undertakes to fetch him. He has to be rescued from a life which is both immortal and unremunerative.

Strether is a typical James character—he recurs in nearly all the books and is an essential part of their construction. He is the observer who tries to influence the action, and who through his failure to do so gains extra opportunities for observation. And the other characters are such as an observer like Strether is capable of observing—through lenses procured from a rather too first-class oculist. Everything is adjusted to his vision, yet he is not a quietist—no, that is the strength of the device; he takes us along with him, we move as well as look on.

When he lands in England (and a landing is an exalted and enduring experience for James, it is as vital as Newgate for Defoe; poetry and life crowd round a landing): when Strether lands, though it is only old England, he begins to have doubts of his mission, which increase when he gets to Paris. For Chad Newsome, far from going to the bad, has improved; he is distinguished, he is so sure of himself that he can be kind and cordial to the man who has orders to fetch him away; his friends are exquisite, and as for "women in the case" whom his mother anticipated, there is no sign of them whatever. It is Paris that has enlarged and redeemed him—and how well Strether himself understands this!

> His greatest uneasiness seemed to peep at him out of the possible impression that almost any acceptance of Paris might give one's authority away. It hung before him this morning, the vast bright Babylon, like some huge iridescent object, a jewel brilliant and hard, in which parts were not to be discriminated nor differences comfortably marked. It twinkled and trembled and melted together; and what seemed all surface one moment seemed all depth the next. It was a place of which, unmistakably, Chad was fond; wherefore, if he, Strether, should like it too much, what on earth, with such a bond, would become of either of them?

Thus, exquisitely and firmly, James sets his atmosphere—Paris irradiates the book from end to end, it is an actor though always unembodied, it is a scale by which human sensibility can be measured, and when we have finished the novel and allow its incidents to blur that we may see the pattern plainer, it is Paris that gleams at the centre of the hour-glass shape—Paris—nothing so crude as good or evil. Strether sees this soon, and sees that Chad realizes it better than he himself can; and when he has reached this stage of initiation the novel takes a turn: there is, after all, a woman in the case; behind Paris, interpreting it for Chad, is the adorable and exalted figure of Mme. de Vionnet. It is now impossible for Strether to proceed. All that is noble and refined in life concentrates in Mme. de Vionnet and is reinforced by her pathos. She asks him not to take Chad away. He promises—without reluctance, for his own heart has already shown him as much—and he remains in Paris not to fight it but to fight for it.

For the second batch of ambassadors now arrives from the New World. Mrs. Newsome, incensed and puzzled by the unseemly delay, has dispatched Chad's sister, his brother-in-law, and Mamie, the girl whom he is supposed to marry. The novel now becomes, within its ordained limits, most amusing. There is a superb set-to between Chad's sister and Mme. de Vionnet, while as for Mamie—here is disastrous Mamie, seen as we see all things, through Strether's eyes.

As a child, as a "bud," and then again as a flower of expansion, Mamie had bloomed for him, freely, in the almost incessantly open doorways of home; where he remembered her at first very forward, as then very backward—for he had carried on at one period, in Mrs. Newsome's parlours, a course of English literature reinforced by exams and teas—and once more, finally, as very much in advance. But he had kept no great sense of points of contact; it not being in the nature of things at Woollett that the freshest of the buds should find herself in the same basket with the most withered of the winter apples. . . . He none the less felt now, as he sat with the charming girl, the signal growth of a confidence. For she *was* charming, when all was said, and none the less so for the visible habit and practice of freedom and fluency. She was charming, he was aware, in spite of the fact that if he hadn't found her so he would have found her something he should have been in peril of expressing as "funny." Yes, she was funny, wonderful Mamie, and without dreaming it; she was bland, she was bridal—with never, that he could make out as yet, a bridegroom to support it; she was handsome and portly, and easy and chatty, soft and sweet and almost disconcertingly reassuring. She was dressed, if we might so far discriminate, less as a young lady than as an old one—had an old one been supposable to Strether as so committed to vanity; the complexities of her hair missed moreover also the looseness of youth; and she had a mature manner of bending a little, as to encourage and reward, while she held neatly in front of her a pair of strikingly polished hands: the combination of all of which kept up about her the glamour of her "receiving," placed her again perpetually between the windows and within sound of the ice cream plates, suggested the enumeration of all the names, gregarious specimens of a single type, she was happy to "meet."

Mamie! She is another Henry James type; nearly every novel contains a Mamie—Mrs. Gereth in *The Spoils of Poynton* for instance, or Henrietta Stackpole in *The Portrait of a Lady*. He is so good at indicating instantaneously and constantly that a character is second-rate, deficient in sensitiveness, abounding in the wrong sort of worldliness; he gives such a character so much vitality that its absurdity is delightful.

So Strether changes sides and loses all hopes of

marrying Mrs. Newsome. Paris is winning—and then he catches sight of something new. Is not Chad, as regards any fineness in him, played out? Is not Chad's Paris after all just a place for a spree? This fear is confirmed. He goes for a solitary country walk, and at the end of the day he comes across Chad and Mme. de Vionnet. They are in a boat, they pretend not to see him, because their relation is at bottom an ordinary liaison, and they are ashamed. They were hoping for a secret week-end at an inn while their passion survived; for it will not survive, Chad will tire of the exquisite Frenchwoman, she is part of his fling; he will go back to his mother and make the little domestic article and marry Mamie. They know all this, and it is revealed to Strether though they try to hide it; they lie, they are vulgar—even Mme. de Vionnet, even her pathos, once so exquisite, is stained with commonness.

It was like a chill in the air to him, it was almost appalling, that a creature so fine could be, by mysterious forces, a creature so exploited. For, at the end of all things, they *were* mysterious; she had but made Chad what he was—so why could she think she had made him infinite? She had made him better, she had made him best, she had made him anything one would; but it came to our friend with supreme queerness that he was none the less only Chad. The work, however admirable, was nevertheless of the strict human order, and in short it was marvellous that the companion of mere earthly joys, of comforts, aberrations—however one classed them—within the common experience, should be so transcendently prized.

She was older for him tonight, visibly less exempt from the touch of time; but she was as much as ever the finest and subtlest creature, the happiest apparition, it had been given him, in all his years, to meet; and yet he could see her there as vulgarly troubled, in very truth, as a maidservant crying for a young man. The only thing was that she judged herself as the maidservant wouldn't; the weakness of which wisdom too, the dishonour of which judgment, seemed but to sink her lower.

So Strether loses them too. As he says: "I have lost everything—it is my only logic." It is not that they have gone back. It is that he has gone on. The Paris they revealed to him—he could reveal it to them now, if they had eyes to see, for it is something finer than they could ever notice for themselves, and his imagination has more spiritual value than their youth. The pattern of the hour-glass is complete; he and Chad have changed places, with more subtle steps than Thais and Paphnuce, and the light in the clouds proceeds not from the well-lit Alexandria, but from the jewel which "twinkled and trembled and melted together, and what seemed all surface one moment seemed all depth the next."

The beauty that suffuses *The Ambassadors* is the reward due to a fine artist for hard work. James knew exactly what he wanted, he pursued the narrow path of aesthetic duty, and success to the full extent of his possibilities has crowned him. The pattern has woven itself with modulation and reservations Anatole France will never attain. Woven itself wonderfully. But at what sacrifice!

So enormous is the sacrifice that many readers cannot get interested in James, although they can follow what he says (his difficulty has been much exaggerated), and can appreciate his effects. They cannot grant his premise, which is that most of human life has to disappear before he can do us a novel.

He has, in the first place, a very short list of characters. I have already mentioned two—the observer who tries to influence the action, and the second-rate outsider (to whom, for example, all the brilliant opening of *What Maisie Knew* is entrusted). Then there is the sympathetic foil—very lively and frequently female—in *The Ambassadors.* Maria Gostrey plays this part; there is the wonderful rare heroine, whom Mme. de Vionnet approached and who is consummated by Milly in *The Wings of the Dove;* there is sometimes a villain, sometimes a young artist with generous impulses; and that is about all. For so fine a novelist it is a poor show.

In the second place, the characters, beside being few in number, are constructed on very stingy lines. They are incapable of fun, of rapid motion, of carnality, and of nine-tenths of heroism. Their clothes will not take off, the diseases that ravage them are anonymous, like the sources of their income, their servants are noiseless or resemble themselves, no social explanation of the world we know is possible for them, for there are no stupid people in their world, no barriers of language, and no poor. Even their sensations are limited. They can land in Europe and look at works of art and at each other, but that is all. Maimed creatures can alone breathe in Henry

James's pages—maimed yet specialized. They remind one of the exquisite deformities who haunted Egyptian art in the reign of Akhenaton—huge heads and tiny legs, but nevertheless charming. In the following reign they disappear.

Now this drastic curtailment, both of the numbers of human beings and of their attributes, is in the interests of the pattern. The longer James worked, the more convinced he grew that a novel should be a whole—not necessarily geometric like *The Ambassadors,* but it should accrete round a single topic, situation, gesture, which should occupy the characters and provide a plot, and should also fasten up the novel on the outside—catch its scattered statements in a net, make them cohere like a planet, and swing through the skies of memory. A pattern must emerge, and anything that emerged from the pattern must be pruned off as wanton distraction. Who so wanton as human beings? Put Tom Jones or Emma or even Mr. Casaubon into a Henry James book, and the book will burn to ashes, whereas we could put them into one another's books and only cause local inflammation. Only a Henry James character will suit, and though they are not dead—certain selected recesses of experience he explores very well—they are gutted of the common stuff that fills characters in other books, and ourselves. And this castrating is not in the interests of the Kingdom of Heaven, there is no philosophy in the novels, no religion (except an occasional touch of superstition), no prophecy, no benefit for the superhuman at all. It is for the sake of a particular aesthetic effect which is certainly gained, but at this heavy price.

H. G. Wells has been amusing on this point, and perhaps profound. In *Boon*—one of his liveliest works—he had Henry James much upon his mind, and wrote a superb parody of him.

> James begins by taking it for granted that a novel is a work of art that must be judged by its oneness. Some one gave him that idea in the beginning of things and he has never found it out. He doesn't find things out. He doesn't even seem to want to find things out. He accepts very readily and then—elaborates. . . . The only living human motives left in his novels are a certain avidity and an entirely superficial curiosity. . . . His people nose out suspicions, hint by hint, link by link. Have you ever known living human beings do that? The thing his novel is *about* is always there. It is like a church lit but with no congregation to distract you, with every light and line focussed on the high altar. And on the altar, very reverently placed, intensely there, is a dead kitten, an egg shell, a piece of string. . . . Like his *Altar of the Dead* with nothing to the dead at all. . . . For if there was, they couldn't all be candles, and the effect would vanish.

Wells sent *Boon* as a present to James, apparently thinking the master would be as much pleased by such heartiness and honesty as was he himself. The master was far from pleased, and a most interesting correspondence ensued.[1] Each of the eminent men becomes more and more himself as it proceeds. James is polite, reminiscent, bewildered, and exceedingly

[1] See the *Letters of H. James,* Vol. II.

formidable: he admits that the parody has not "filled him with a fond elation," and regrets in conclusion that he can sign himself "only yours faithfully, Henry James." Wells is bewildered too, but in a different way; he cannot understand why the man should be upset. And, beyond the personal comedy, there is the great literary importance of the issue. It is this question of the rigid pattern: hour-glass or grand chain or converging lines of the cathedral or diverging lines of the Catherine wheel, or bed of Procrustes—whatever image you like as long as it implies unity. Can it be combined with the immense richness of material which life provides? Wells and James would agree it cannot, Wells would go on to say that life should be given the preference, and must not be whittled or distended for a pattern's sake. My own prejudices are with Wells. The James novels are a unique possession and the reader who cannot accept his premises misses some valuable and exquisite sensations. But I do not want more of his novels, especially when they are written by someone else, just as I do not want the art of Akhenaton to extend into the reign of Tutankhamen.

That then is the disadvantage of a rigid pattern. It may externalize the atmosphere, spring naturally from the plot, but it shuts the doors on life and leaves the novelist doing exercises, generally in the drawing-room. Beauty has arrived, but in too tyrannous a guise. In plays—the plays of Racine, for instance—she may be justified because beauty can be a great empress on the stage, and reconcile us to the loss of the men we knew. But in the novel, her tyranny as it grows powerful grows petty, and generates regrets which sometimes take the form of books like *Boon.* To put it in other words, the novel is not capable of as much artistic development as the drama: its humanity or the grossness of its material hinder it (use whichever phrase you like). To most readers of fiction the sensation from a pattern is not intense enough to justify the sacrifices that made it, and their verdict is "Beautifully done, but not worth doing."

Still this is not the end of our quest. We will not give up the hope of beauty yet. Cannot it be introduced into fiction by some other method than the pattern? Let us edge rather nervously towards the idea of "rhythm."

Rhythm is sometimes quite easy. Beethoven's Fifth Symphony, for instance, starts with the rhythm "diddidy dum," which we can all hear and tap to. But the symphony as a whole has also a rhythm—due mainly to the relation between its movements—which some people can hear but no one can tap to. This second sort of rhythm is difficult, and whether it is substantially the same as the first sort only a musician could tell us. What a literary man wants to say though is that the first kind of rhythm, the diddidy dum, can be found in certain novels and may give them beauty. And the other rhythm, the difficult one—the rhythm of the Fifth Symphony as a whole—I cannot quote you any parallels for that in fiction, yet it may be present.

Rhythm in the easy sense, is illustrated by the work of Marcel Proust.[1]

Proust's conclusion has not been published yet, and his admirers say that when it comes everything will fall into its place, times past will be recaptured and fixed, we shall have a perfect whole. I do not believe this. The work seems to me a progressive rather than an aesthetic confession, and with the elaboration of Albertine the author was getting tired. Bits of news may await us, but it will be surprising if we have to revise our opinion of the whole book. The book is chaotic, ill-constructed, it has and will have no external shape; and yet it hangs together because it is stitched internally, because it contains rhythms.

There are several examples (the photographing of the grandmother is one of them) but the most important from the binding point of view is his use of the "little phrase" in the music of Vinteuil. It does more than anything else—more even than the jealousy which successively destroys Swann, the hero, and Charlus—to make us feel that we are in a homogeneous world. We first hear Vinteuil's name in hideous circumstances. The musician is dead—an obscure little country organist, unknown to fame—and his daughter is defiling his memory. The horrible scene is to radiate in several directions, but it passes, we forget about it.

[1] The first three books of *A la recherche du temps perdu* have been excellently translated by C. K. Scott Moncrieff under the title of *Remembrance of Things Past,* A. & C. Boni.

Then we are at a Paris salon. A violin sonata is performed and a little phrase from its andante catches the ear of Swann and steals into his life. It is always a living being, but takes various forms. For a time it attends his love for Odette. The love affair goes wrong, the phrase is forgotten, we forget it. Then it breaks out again when he is ravaged by jealousy, and now it attends his misery and past happiness at once, without losing its own divine character. Who wrote the sonata? On hearing it is by Vinteuil, Swann says, "I once knew a wretched little organist of that name—it couldn't be by him." But it is, and Vinteuil's daughter and her friend transcribed and published it.

That seems all. The little phrase crosses the book again and again, but as an echo, a memory; we like to encounter it, but it has no binding power. Then, hundreds and hundreds of pages on, when Vinteuil has become a national possession, and there is talk of raising a statue to him in the town where he has been so wretched and so obscure, another work of his is performed—a posthumous sextet. The hero listens—he is in an unknown rather terrible universe while a sinister dawn reddens the sea. Suddenly for him and for the reader too, the little phrase of the sonata recurs—half heard, changed, but giving complete orientation, so that he is back in the country of his childhood with the knowledge that it belongs to the unknown.

We are not obliged to agree with Proust's actual musical descriptions (they are too pictorial for my own taste): but what we must admire is his use of rhythm in literature, and his use of something which is akin by nature to the effect it has to produce—namely a musical phrase. Heard by various people—first by Swann, then by the hero—the phrase of Vinteuil is not tethered; it is not a banner such as we find George Meredith using—a double-blossomed cherry tree to accompany Clara Middleton, a yacht in smooth waters for Cecilia Halkett. A banner can only reappear, rhythm can develop, and the little phrase has a life of its own, unconnected with the lives of its auditors, as with the life of the man who composed it. It is almost an actor, but not quite, and that "not quite" means that its power has gone towards stitching Proust's book together from the inside, and towards the establishment of beauty and the ravishing of the reader's memory. There are times when the little phrase—from its gloomy inception, through the sonata into the sextet—means everything to the reader. There are times when it means nothing and is forgotten, and this seems to me the function of rhythm in fiction; not to be there all the time like a pattern, but by its lovely waxing and waning to fill us with surprise and freshness and hope.

Done badly, rhythm is most boring, it hardens into a symbol and instead of carrying us on it trips us up. With exasperation we find that Galsworthy's spaniel John, or whatever it is, lies under the feet again; and even Meredith's cherry trees and yachts, graceful as they are, only open the windows into poetry. I doubt that it can be achieved by the writers who plan their books beforehand, it has to depend on a local impulse when the right interval is reached. But the effect can be exquisite, it can be obtained without mutilating the characters, and it lessens our need of an external form.

That must suffice on the subject of easy rhythm in fiction: which may be defined as repetition plus variation, and which can be illustrated by examples. Now for the more difficult question. Is there any effect in novels comparable to the effect of the Fifth Symphony as a whole, where, when the orchestra stops, we hear something that has never actually been played? The opening movement, the andante, and the trio-scherzo-trio-finale-trio-finale that composes the third block, all enter the mind at once, and extend one another into a common entity. This common entity, this new thing, is the symphony as a whole, and it has been achieved mainly (though not entirely) by the relation between the three big blocks of sound which the orchestra has been playing. I am calling this relation "rhythmic." If the correct musical term is something else, that does not matter; what we have now to ask ourselves is whether there is any analogy to it in fiction.

I cannot find any analogy. Yet there may be one; in music fiction is likely to find its nearest parallel.

The position of the drama is different. The drama may look towards the pictorial arts, it may allow Aristotle to discipline it, for it is not so deeply committed to the claims of human beings. Human beings have their great chance in the novel. They say to the novelist: "Recreate us if you like, but we must come in," and the novelist's problem, as we have seen all along, is to give them a good run and to achieve something else at the same time. Whither shall he turn? not indeed for help but for analogy. Music, though it does not employ human beings, though it is governed by intricate laws, nevertheless does offer in its final expression a type of beauty which fiction might achieve in its own way. Expansion. That is the idea the novelist must cling to. Not completion. Not rounding off but opening out. When the symphony is over we feel that the notes and tunes composing it have been liberated, they have found in the rhythm of the whole their individual freedom. Cannot the novel be like that? Is not there something of it in *War and Peace*?—the book with which we began and in which we must end. Such an untidy book. Yet, as we read it, do not great chords begin to sound behind us, and when we have finished does not every item—even the catalogue of strategies—lead a larger existence than was possible at the time?

Nine

CONCLUSION

It is tempting to conclude by speculations as to the future of the novel, will it become more or less realistic, will it be killed by the cinema, and so on. Speculations, whether sad or lively, always have a large air about them, they are a very convenient way of being helpful or impressive. But we have no right to entertain them. We have refused to be hampered by the past, so we must not profit by the future. We have visualized the novelists of the last two hundred years all writing together in one room, subject to the same emotions and putting the accidents of their age into the crucible of inspiration, and whatever our results, our method has been sound—sound for an assemblage of pseudo-scholars like ourselves. But we must visualize the novelists of the next two hundred years as also writing in the room. The change in their subject matter will be enormous; they will not change. We may harness the atom, we may land on the moon, we may abolish or intensify warfare, the mental processes of animals may be understood; but all these are trifles, they belong to history not to art. History develops, art stands still. The novelist of the future will have to pass all the new facts through the old if variable mechanism of the creative mind.

There is however one question which touches our subject, and which only a psychologist could answer. But let us ask it. Will the creative process itself alter? Will the mirror get a new coat of quicksilver? In other words, can human nature change? Let us consider this possibility for a moment—we are entitled to that much relaxation.

It is amusing to listen to elderly people on this subject. Sometimes a man says in confident tones. "Human nature's the same in all ages. The primitive cave man lies deep in us all. Civilization—pooh! a mere veneer. You can't alter facts." He speaks like this when he is feeling prosperous and fat. When he is feeling depressed and is worried by the young, or is being sentimental about them on the ground that they will succeed in life when he has failed, then he will take the opposite view and say mysteriously, "Human nature is not the same. I have seen fundamental changes in my own time. You must face facts." And he goes on like this day after day, alternately facing facts and refusing to alter them.

All I will do is to state a possibility. If human nature does alter it will be because individuals manage to look at themselves in a new way. Here and there people—a very few people, but a few novelists are among them—are trying to do this. Every institution and vested interest is against such a search: organized religion, the state, the family in its economic aspect, have nothing to gain, and it is only when outward prohibitions weaken that it can proceed: history conditions it to that extent. Perhaps the searchers will fail, perhaps it is impossible for the instrument of contemplation to contemplate itself, perhaps if it is possible it means the end of imaginative literature—which if I understand him rightly is the view of that acute inquirer, Mr. I. A. Richards. Anyhow—that way lies movement and even combustion for the novel, for if the novelist sees himself differently he will see his characters differently and a new system of lighting will result.

I do not know on the verge of which philosophy or what rival philosophies the above remarks are wavering, but as I look back at my own scraps of knowledge and into my own heart, I see these two movements of the human mind: the great tedious onrush known as history, and a shy crablike sideways movement. Both movements have been neglected in these lectures: history because it only carries people on, it is just a train full of passengers; and the crablike movement because it is too slow and cautious to be visible over our tiny period of two hundred years. So we laid it down as an axiom when we started that human nature is unchangeable, and that it produces in rapid succession prose fictions, which fictions, when they contain 50,000 words or more, are called novels. If we had the power or license to take a wider view, and survey all human and pre-human activity, we might not conclude like this; the crablike movement, the shiftings of the passengers, might be visible, and the phrase "the development of the novel" might cease to be a pseudo-scholarly tag or a technical triviality, and become important, because it implied the development of humanity.

Index of Main References

Books by E. M. Forster
available in Harvest paperback editions
from Harcourt Brace & Company

ABINGER HARVEST

ASPECTS OF THE NOVEL

THE ETERNAL MOMENT AND OTHER STORIES

THE HILL OF DEVI

A PASSAGE TO INDIA

TWO CHEERS FOR DEMOCRACY